12

WOMEN, HISTORY, & THEORY

Women in Culture and Society
A Series Edited by Catharine R. Stimpson

JOAN KELLY

Women, history & theory

The Essays of Joan Kelly

The University of Chicago Press
Chicago & London

Until the late 1970s, Joan Kelly published as Joan Kelly-Gadol. This volume uses the name she ultimately preferred.

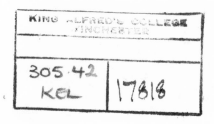
The University of Chicago Press, Chicago 60637
The University of Chicago Press, Ltd., London

© 1984 by The University of Chicago
All rights reserved. Published 1984
Printed in the United States of America

93 92 91 90 89 88 87 86 85 84   54321

Library of Congress Cataloging in Publication Data
Kelly, Joan, 1928–1982.
    Women, history, and theory.

    (Women in culture and society)
    Includes index.
    Contents: The social relation of the sexes—Did women have a Renaissance?—The doubled vision of feminist theory—[etc.]
    1. Feminism—Addresses, essays, lectures.
    2. Women—History—Addresses, essays, lectures.
    I. Title. II. Series.
    HQ1154.K38   1984   305.4′09   84-2558
    ISBN 0-226-43027-8

I dedicate this book to all my sisters,
and to each of them

CONTENTS

FOREWORD

*J*oan Kelly's place in scholarship is distinguished. She was a special member of the generation that first developed the contemporary study of women. In the 1960s, she had been a Renaissance historian, trained at Columbia University. Then, in the 1970s, she moved from that field to take on the new subject of women. Her change altered the history of the Renaissance and shaped that of women.

Her influence has been pervasive and exhilarating. Perhaps most usefully, she constructed a "vantage point," a common phrase in her writing, from which to regard women and history. Her essays draft and redraft that perspective. She looked simultaneously at public and private spheres and at their linkages. In so doing, she synthesized several intellectual traditions. She drew, for example, on Marxist thought for her understanding of work; on emerging feminist theory for her sense of the family and sexuality.

Kelly thought boldly, but never arrogantly. She hoped that the study of women would prove powerful enough to stimulate future generations to test, refine, and revise her ideas. Though an exemplary and charismatic figure, she believed that her scholarship was part of a collaborative effort, done in the present for the sake of the future.

In August 1982, she died of cancer. She was fifty-four. Before her death, she had contracted with the University of Chicago Press, the publisher of her first book, to produce a volume about women, history, and theory. When she realized she would not finish it, she planned what we have here.

This book begins with an Introduction, which five trusted friends and colleagues wrote after her death. Her most significant essays are next: "The Social Relation of the Sexes" (1976), "Did Women Have a Renaissance?" (1977), "The Doubled Vision of Feminist Theory" (1979), and "Early Feminist Theory and the *Querelle des Femmes*" (1982). The first three appear as they were published. The fourth was originally printed in a shortened version. It has now been edited, as she wished, only to delete redundancies and errors she herself would have erased. The book's final section is an essay retitled "Family and Society." Lucid, sweeping, it was designed for a general, not a scholarly, audience. It shows Kelly as a teacher, a pedagogue, and a synthesizer of fact and theory.

Joan Kelly's own words introduce her essays. During the last months of her life, Kelly dictated a series of tapes. In effect they were notes for the readers of this book. I have edited their transcripts into the Author's Preface and the introduction to the final essay, "Family and Society."

I am indebted to many people for their help: Blanche Wiesen Cook, Clare Coss, Moira Ferguson, Martin Fleisher, Alice Kessler Harris, Carolyn Lougee, Rosalind P. Petchesky, and Amy Swerdlow. We are all grateful to Joan Kelly for her faith that we would bring her book to its proper conclusion. It is posthumous, but our gallant, brilliant precursor is alive in print and memory.

Catharine R. Stimpson

AUTHOR'S PREFACE

*T*he essays gathered together in this volume were written or begun in the 1970s. The women's movement was forcing new insights upon us, raising queries about what we thought we knew so well, and disturbing us with a sense of ignorance and inadequacy about our own past. Some of the essays were to be delivered at conferences. Others were commissioned. Still others were intended as sections of a larger book about feminist theory.[1] Some are chiefly historical, others more theoretical. No matter what their shape, size, or intention, they are all of a piece. They form for me, and I hope for the reader, a coherent statement that has to do not so much with the particular content of an essay as with points discovered and elaborated upon, as with perspective.

The idea of feminism as a vantage point was, indeed, one of my first and enduring discoveries. I had come to women's history after years of training and practice, teaching and writing, as a European historian, particularly of Renaissance Italy. Even there, perspective was one of my major concerns. My book on Leon Battista Alberti (1404–72) dealt with painter's perspective, which Alberti had done so much to develop.[2] Alberti flourished a generation before Leonardo and was very much of his type. Yet, unlike Leonardo, he was a skilled classicist, humanist, and

poet. I discovered how painter's perspective and the elementary
ideas connected with it—of measure, proportion, harmony, and
scale—constituted a key to Alberti and to the major changes in
the fifteenth and sixteenth centuries in the perceptual organization of the world. The discovery of new pictorial, geographical,
and astronomical worlds expressed this new orientation of perception and thought. It explains why a painter, like Leonardo,
should be a mapmaker as well as an astronomer; why a Kepler,
who developed new laws of plantetary motion, should be absorbed by Pythagorean issues and the harmony of the spheres.
Accompanying the enormous social, economic, and political
transformations of feudal into early modern society was a comprehensive intellectual transformation that brought about a new
heaven and sense of human destiny. There emerged a newly
harmonious order in which everything was commensurate with
everything else. The rational capacities of man could measure all.

Having taught, studied, and written about this new perspective, this great transformation, for a decade or more, I was pre-
pared intellectually to appreciate what women's history, women's
studies, feminist scholarship would or could mean. By the time
my book on Alberti was published in 1969, I was caught up in
the excitement of the women's movement. Yet, in no way had
my first feminist interests affected my work. It is a long way
from intellectual preparedness and social action to full consciousness. Before my intellectual and personal life could cohere,
I had to go through an exciting transformation of consciousness
such as I had once described, but now was to experience. If
I have emphasized how feminism is a perspective on social reality as well as a social movement, it is because I underwent
that change of consciousness so dramatically—and so self-
consciously.

By 1971, I was teaching at Sarah Lawrence College. Gerda
Lerner, a pioneer in women's history, wrote to members of
the faculty asking her colleagues to participate in developing
courses, programs, or even a lecture about women in relation to
their fields. I remember dropping her a note, commending her
for her interests but saying that since I was in Renaissance history, there was nothing much I could offer about women. She
telephoned, insisted upon meeting me, and talked for well over

four hours on the almost infinite possibilities that lay ahead of me in women's history—considering that I was indeed a Renaissance historian. I was not convinced by what she said, but I was struck by the forcefulness and intelligence with which she said it. I promised that for the coming weekend, I would think of my field and what I knew in relation to women.

That turned out to be the most exciting intellectual adventure I can recall. It was like a very rapid repetition of the confusion into which I had been plunged in adolescence: the profoundly frightening feeling of all coherence gone, followed by restoration, if not of a new order, at least of a new direction. Suddenly, the entire world of learning was open to me. It had a new and compelling attraction and was utterly questionable at the same time. Most compelling, and most questionable, was everything I thought I had known about the Renaissance.

The change I went through was kaleidoscopic. I had not read a new book. I did not stumble upon a new archive. No fresh piece of information was added to anything I knew. But I knew now that the entire picture I had held of the Renaissance was partial, distorted, limited, and deeply flawed by those limitations. Leonardo had said that "the earth is not in the center of the sun's orbit nor at the center of the universe . . . and anyone standing on the moon, when it and the sun are both beneath us, would see this our earth and the element of water upon it just as we see the moon (*et es luminus*), and the earth would light it [the moon] as it lights us." All I had done was to say, with Leonardo, suppose we look at the dark, dense immobile earth from the vantage point of the moon? Suppose we look again at this age, the Renaissance, reputed for its liberation from old and confining forms, renowned for its revival of classical and republican ideas? Suppose we look at the Renaissance from the vantage point of women?

Because of my illness, if this book were to appear at all, the preparation of it had to fall on other people. Nothing guaranteed that anyone would respond to this need except out of a sense of sisterhood and love. I believe all feminist work emerges out of the spirit and reality of collectivity. Mine has. When women are scattered and cannot work together, a condition that originated with the early modern state, women suffer a loss in position and in the possibility of feminist expression. When some connection among women exists, even if it is only a literary one (as it was among the participants in the *querelle des femmes*), it creates an impressive tradition of feminist thinking. My essays were first reviewed by friends, whom I acknowledge in the notes of each article.

The idea of collecting my essays was Kate Stimpson's. I am grateful to her. I also want to thank my friends—Clare Coss, Blanche Wiesen Cook, Alice Kessler Harris, Rosalind Petchesky, Amy Swerdlow, and, of course, my husband, Martin Fleisher.

Thank you very much, dear friends.

Joan Kelly

Notes

1. I would like to thank the National Endowment for the Humanities for a research fellowship in 1980–81 that supported elements of my work.

2. Joan Kelly-Gadol, *Leon Battista Alberti: Universal Man of the Early Renaissance* (Chicago: University of Chicago Press, 1969); "Universal Man," *Dictionary of the History of Ideas* (New York: Charles Scribner's, 1973); "Alberti," *Encyclopaedia Brittanica* (1974). See, too, "The Unity of the Renaissance: Humanism, Natural Science, and Art," in *Renaissance to the Counter-Reformation: Essays in Honor of Garrett Mattingly* (New York: Random House, 1965), pp. 29–55.

INTRODUCTION

*I*can read, and do, Charlotte Perkins Gilman and feel my life connect with hers, my cause with hers. Hope I can contribute as she did; know I have, but I now want to do more. I want that suffering that we can control to stop, it outrages and tears at me, the cruel and stupid political world. And I want women's indignities to be ended—millennia long, borne with such endurance and grace. I want, what I really want, and now great pleasure comes through me: I want our day to come. I want women to take the lead. And I know, in the depth of my being and in all my knowledge of history and humanity, I know women will struggle for a social order of peace, equality, joy. Women will make the world concern itself with children. Our problem is, how do we "make" the world do that? Oh, I want an end to patriarchy! Passionately!
—Joan Kelly's *Cancer Journal* (1982)

Joan Kelly devoted her intellectual life to the understanding of consciousness, its roots, and its power to effect social change. Her life was a feminist self-creation—a work of thought and feeling, of scholarship and experience—in the pursuit of sisterhood and community. Feminism for Kelly meant a total transformation of self as well as society. She came to feminism out of the political struggles and social tensions of the 1960s. Trained in Renaissance history, she was a professor at the City University of New York for twenty-six years. Her attentiveness to the concerns of her students and her own humanism and sense of justice impelled her to be one of the first faculty members at City College to join students in demonstrations against racial discrimination and the war in Indochina. She supported demands of minority students for an open admissions policy at City University, led her colleagues to work for the appointment of faculty members conversant with new perspectives of social history, and pioneered in fresh approaches to teaching. Her active participation in the civil rights and anti–Vietnam War movements deepened her understanding of the connections between race, class, and sexual oppression. These concerns and activities led her to the women's liberation movement of the late 1960s. She was a leader in the struggle of women historians for recognition and equality and in the movement for reproductive rights and codirected the Women's Studies Program at Sarah Lawrence College.

Kelly saw her scholarly work as more than an individual quest for knowledge and understanding: it was part of a collective process to be shared in both its creation and its dissemination. The substantial part of her time she devoted to collective study and action groups resulted in such contributions as the *Workbook on Sterilization and Sterilization Abuse*; a feminist family text, *Household and Kin*; and a bibliography in European women's history. In addition, she helped to create two institutes on integrating women's history into the high school curriculum, she participated for many years in a Marxist-feminist discussion group, and she cotaught numerous women's studies courses. During the last years of her life, she described how she felt energized by the "incredible women's network that connected me to myself and my sisters."

For Kelly politics was everywhere. It involved more than active opposition to economic injustice, sexism, racism, and to hierarchical relationships in the larger society and in the university; it involved both writing and teaching. Kelly had a gift for making students and colleagues feel empowered by her belief in their capacities for important, effective life-enhancing work. A member of her 1973 freshman studies class in European women's history at Sarah Lawrence College described this process: "As a class we were a community of scholars, individuals pursuing, with the same integrity and love, separate interests, which through our pursuits and sharing could only deepen our understanding of ourselves as individuals and as members of that community. The respect we learned to have for one another's work was a transmission of the respect we felt Joan had for us."

Kelly herself wrote of the last feminist theory seminar she taught at the CUNY graduate center,

> I've worked out a teaching style that would have fostered me . . . and I'm convinced that it's the form for feminist and socialist growth. The students do the work, though I plan it, guide it, and . . . bring in those really central (I think) points at a time when everyone can take it in. . . . I get excited about the feminist ideas again, and I feel it in my writing and vice versa. I am energized by it, and like the sense of who I am and what I do.

Teaching for Kelly was part of learning and sharing, involving commitment and trust from both student and teacher. The last essay in this book is part of a feminist history of the family written for high school students. Kelly gave her energy and enthusiasm to this collaborative work because she believed that every generation has to find its own way to shape its own institutions, and that only through a knowledge of social process and the variety of family structures that human beings have devised over time would young people today have a sense of their own personal and social possibilities. In her 1976 commencement address at Sarah Lawrence College, she told the graduates:

> Our social institutions allow us to express and share so little of our real human needs that we are forced to lock them up inside ourselves. We all bear witness to the results: the explosions and implosions of these pent-up feelings are the stuff of the private tragedies and public violence and the disorder of our everyday life. Let us acknowledge, then . . . that the personal is political; that the test of a social system is its ability to translate the personal into the public and at the same time to make community a real part of one's daily, personal life through meaningful participation in the decisions that shape us all.

Kelly's feminist vision had been prefigured in her earlier work on the Renaissance. The subject of her first major book, Leon Battista Alberti, appealed to Kelly because his life joined practice and theory; blended artistic, technical, and humanist concerns; and reflected a commitment to reason, harmony, and inspired intuition. He appeared to Kelly as an extraordinary spirit of the time whose life seemed to bear out his own youthful conviction that "nothing is too difficult for study and determination to overcome." She was not only impressed by Alberti's "versatility and determination to excel" but attracted to another outstanding trait: "That which others created he welcomed joyfully, . . . and [he] held every human achievement which followed the laws of beauty for something almost divine." The most significant question asked by Renaissance humanists such as Alberti was, How do we perceive our world, from what perspective, which vantage point? Once asked, that question leads in many directions at once. Like the Renaissance humanists committed to perspectival reorganization, Kelly's goal was to achieve a level of consciousness about the psyche, the economy, the process of creativity that would render new patterns of living accessible.

Kelly's intellectual and theoretical transformation from Renaissance scholar to feminist scholar encompassed every mode of being. Music, literature, art, architecture, and society were the ongoing subjects of her inquiry. Only her perspective changed. Feminism required another look at the nature of the "universalist" theme of the Renaissance. Her task was not unlike Alberti's. Where he asked how humanists perceive and create a coherent moral metaphysical pattern of understanding out of the alienating and crumbling structures of medieval society, she asked how feminists might confront a misogynist society. For Kelly feminism was "a perspective on social reality as well as a social movement."

To shift the perspective, to adjust the vantage point, creates new contours, possibilities, and realities. To look at the Renaissance from the perspective of women exploded all previous understanding about women in history. Even the universalist view of society, so central to Renaissance thought, required reordering. To refocus the prism to show the role and place of women in the Renaissance made Kelly "acutely aware of the need to

supplement this 'universalist' view which, ironically, is too limited, too one-dimensional, for historical truth." Renaissance
women were not, Kelly recognized, "on a footing of perfect
equality with men." In her early article, "Women in the Renaissance and Renaissance Historiography," she wrote: "As soon as
we take the emancipation of women as our vantage point, we
discover that events which change the course of history for men,
liberating them from natural, social, or ideological restraints
upon their powers, may have quite different, even opposite
effects upon women."

In Kelly's generative essays on women and the Renaissance,
she transformed the way scholars look at historical society: They
now are called upon to take into account (1) the regulation of female sexuality as compared with male sexuality; (2) women's
economic and political roles and the education needed for work,
property, and power; (3) the cultural role of women in shaping
the outlook of society; and (4) the prevailing ideology about
women. Contrasting the place and conditions of medieval and
Renaissance women, Kelly, in one of her most incisive contributions to our understanding of ideology, noted that

> the sexual nature of courtly love . . . represents an ideologi-
> cal liberation of [feudal women's] sexual and affective powers
> that must have some social reference. This is not to raise the
> fruitless question of whether such love relationships actually
> existed or if they were mere literary conventions. The real
> issue regarding ideology is, rather, what kind of society
> could posit as a social ideal a love relation outside of mar-
> riage, one that women freely entered and that, despite its
> reciprocity, made women the gift givers while men did the
> service. What were the social conditions that fostered these
> particular conventions rather than the more common ones of
> female chastity and/or dependence? ("Did Women Have a
> Renaissance?")

Building upon contemporary feminist theorists, Kelly proposed that we regard "the social relationships of the sexes as a
fundamental category of historical thought." To effect "a new,
systematic relation between men and women, and between the
particular and the universal," was, Kelly wrote, "as fundamental
to the analysis of human history as the social relationship of

classes." Finally, she noted, just as the oppressed make of freedom a social demand, the oppressed, not the oppressor, offers
the true consciousness of a free self and society in which relations of domination no longer obtain.

Issues of access to private and public power, ownership and
control of property, dependence, independence, courage, and
survival remained central concerns in Kelly's research. What
were the conditions, in the state and in the family, that led
women away from independence and self-rule and toward sub-
mission to male authority? In her first full theoretical statement
about women's history, "The Social Relations of the Sexes: Meth-
odological Implications of Women's History," Kelly suggested
three ways in which the kind of question raised by the new history had altered our perceptions of the past. It had encouraged
historians to rethink accepted conventions of periodization and
to reevaluate the notion that Western civilization had moved
from repressive to more liberating structures. A study of women's
status, she noted, revealed that periods of progressive change,
such as the Renaissance and the French Revolution, tended to
subject women to more, not fewer, strictures. Second, women's
history enabled us to include sex, along with race and class, as a
category of analysis. Analyzing women's distinctive relationships to property and production would illuminate not only
their actual social conditions, but also their perception of their
value in society. This new feminist perspective rejects platitudes
about women's natural destiny, substituting instead questions
about the position and function of women in particular times
and places. Finally, Kelly suggested that by integrating class and
sex, women's history transforms our understanding of social
change. She argued that as the domestic and public spheres di-
verged, women increasingly lost control over production, property, and their own persons.

Seeing this process affirmed and intensified Kelly's quest for
an informed Marxist-feminist analysis and moved her toward
new levels of insight. Her integration of Marxism and feminism
took root in an aspect of Marxist tradition that is integrative,
humanistic, and holistic. Her understanding of theory, from
Alberti and the Renaissance, as a "conceptual vision," a perspective or vantage point, made her particularly receptive to the

important stream of Marxism that is continually seeking out the connections between ideas and the social relations in which ideas exist. Along with her passionate identification with women and the long tradition of feminist protest, this intellectual concern with the social roots of ideas—or human consciousness—fired Kelly's own commitment to developing a truly Marxist-feminist theory. For several years this commitment involved a collective feminist study of Marx and Marxism. The collective nature of this intellectual journey was always for her an integral and joyful part of Marxist-feminist politics.

Most of her work as a feminist may be seen as a study of consciousness. A central core of that work was to take the insights of Marxist theory of ideology and apply them to the social relations and ideas of patriarchy, and to its antithesis, feminism. In her analysis of courtly love, for example, she identified a problem only conceivable from a Marxist vantage point but given shape through feminist questions—that is, how to explain the origin of apparently deviant or resistant values in the culture and their function as "ideals." Such values, says Kelly, "must have some social reference," some basis in reality, that would allow (aristocratic) women sexual freedom outside of marriage in a predominantly patriarchal society. Kelly identified a critical issue for any historical period or culture in "Did Women Have a Renaissance," where she explored the tension between women's oppression and their real power. Women's control of courtly love reflected their "actual power" in the medieval aristocracy. At the same time, courtly love functioned as an accommodative ideal which concealed the "tensions between it and other social values," especially patriarchal marriage.

Another respect in which Kelly's feminism was consistently infused with a Marxist vision was her clarity about how gender relations and antagonism are everywhere complicated by the relations of class and race. This understanding acknowledges the specificity of different women's experience of male or patriarchal oppression. The essay "Family and Society" is an analysis of the historical development of "family life," viewed as a spectrum of different class and cultural experiences within a changing framework. Here Kelly distills what is particular for women in contrast to men in each period and in different social groups.

As in all of her essays, she begins by allying herself with the reader. She invites inquiry, analysis, and self-directed conscious-ness, rather than simply providing information or a set of ideas. Kelly wants learning to take place here through a dialectical partnership with her own theoretical process. "For most of us, the family meets many of our needs for love and support. We tend to think that all families do this in the same way. Yet fami-lies are almost as varied as people." She assures us that we are not alone in picturing "the family" to be the imagined universal: a man, a woman, and children. Using anthropological sources she concludes that "the only universal element" about families is that "human beings always form them."

Kelly moves us through a historical perspective of family forms that includes tribal, preindustrial, and industrial societies. She shows how an understanding of the social function of fam-ily systems is integral to each society's organization of produc-tion, division of labor by sex and age, and patterns of child rear-ing. She observes how power relations within the family, gender roles, and attitudes toward sexual behavior affect women. The nuclear family is placed clearly in the context of social produc-tion with the introduction of wage work and the division of fam-ily labor. She graphically describes how the wage relationship affects each member of the nuclear family and reinforces the iso-lation of women. Kelly's understanding of class, race, and sex/gender interconnections led her to see patriarchy itself as emerg-ing out of specific class and historical conditions—not as some static universal category. In this essay, she locates more precisely than any feminist writing before or since the origins of modern patriarchy in the bourgeois and peasant household relations of early modern Europe.

Kelly's Marxist-feminism refocuses our vision toward all the relations of conflict and alienation that keep human potential from being realized. Class, race, and sex/gender divisions con-tinually shape one another; they are both interactive and dis-tinct so that, while all women share a common reality, a com-mon oppression, as well as potential power, their experience is different both within their particular class and because of it.

Kelly elicits this totality most forcefully in "The Doubled Vi-sion of Feminist Theory." The unified "doubled" view of the social order Kelly invoked in her 1979 article, now a classic analysis of feminist thought, was meant to knit together several divided visions. First was the false division within theory between a female sphere of "private" as opposed to a male sphere of "public" activity. Kelly saw this split as ideological, reminding us that "our personal, social, and historical experience is . . . shaped by the simultaneous operation of relations of work and sex, relations that are systematically bound to each other—and always have been so bound." Next was the false division between personal experience and knowledge, the subjective and the objective. To transcend this division, Kelly believed, was feminism's most singular and revolutionary task. "To change our subjective experience," "to restructure how we come to know self and others," is a profoundly political and social undertaking. Finally, there was the need to integrate theory and practice. In "The Doubled Vision," Kelly called on us to bring our feminist values and critique of male dominance into the institutions where we work, teach, and live. "Abolishing all forms of hierarchy," in every domain of power, means practicing feminism wherever we are. For Kelly, the distinctive contribution of feminism to the form and organization of all progressive social movements was its concern with empowering people and democratizing personal relationships.

In the two years before her death, Kelly began to theorize about the historical foundations and contemporary sweep of feminist thought. She was in the process of systematically examining the corpus of feminist ideas from its beginnings. Looking toward a systematic, longitudinal theory of feminism, she had developed a definition of "feminist" that emphasized a consciousness about women that extends beyond individual oppression or exploitation. Kelly's "conceptual vision" of feminism contained the following essential ingredients: it had to be consciously "oppositional," engaged in "a dialectical opposition to misogyny"; and it had to be consciously collective, identifying its struggle as a social one. In the introduction to "Early Feminism and the *Querelle des Femmes*," she describes the early feminists as "literate women who felt themselves and all women maligned" by misogynist ideology. She saw them as "defenders or advocates of women" as a "social group."

At her death, Kelly left behind notes for the early chapters of a book on feminist theory. Unlike the other essays in this volume, "Early Feminism" was conceived as a chapter in this longer work, a historical and theoretical analysis of the systematic connections and differences in past and present antipatriarchal consciousness and feminist thought. Kelly's impulse to recover and analyze the four-hundred-year tradition of women's opposition to male defamation stemmed from her perception that feminist theory was comprehensive and cumulative, with each stage retaining some of the values and limitations of its predecessors. A comprehensive feminist theory, she thought, must go beyond ahistorical, transcultural condemnation of patriarchy to an understanding of its historical specificity, its class relations, and its structural and institutional permutations. Feminist theory, Kelly proposed, emerged at points in history when women living "on the boundary" of male society and culture push beyond traditional consciousness and engage in active struggle. What, she asked, are the conditions that allow an oppositional culture to emerge, and what forces limit its vision so that it still borrows from and relies upon the culture of oppression?

Her important insight in the *Querelle* essay was to see beyond the disconnected polemical responses to misogynist attacks. She discerned a rich, coherent, connected body of feminist thought capable of transmitting to generations of women, who were losing status and power, the knowledge and the confidence they needed to reject claims of female inferiority. In her notes, she weighed some of her earlier insights against a series of problems posed by her attempt to develop a usable theoretical framework. More than in any previous work, her preoccupation is with the nature of consciousness—feminist consciousness in particular, revolutionary or resistant consciousness in general. One feels the influence here of all the strains that made up Joan Kelly's vision: psychoanalysis, Hegelian and Marxist theory, as well as hundreds of years of feminist outrage now informed by the work of contemporary radical feminism.

But changing consciousness, achieving the "doubled vision" that would enable one both to engage in patriarchal society in order to change it and to stand outside it in order to see what must be changed, remains, Kelly knew, a formidable task. Any individual's capacity to make that leap was inhibited by a "divided consciousness" conditioned by patriarchal thought, language, and values. How would one transcend those insidious forms? How do people come to consciousness?

In her notes on feminist theory, Kelly concluded that an oppositional consciousness arises out of its antithesis, out of "the discrepancy between the real and the ideal" experienced by those who stand on the boundary of the dominant culture. Like Hegel's slave, woman experiences an "unhappy consciousness," a form of alienation that makes her at once a participant in the culture that oppresses her and a stranger to it. She is marginal. Out of this marginality arises the possibility of an existential awareness of her situation, and of naming it and opposing it. From the marginality of all women, feminist theory develops. But theory, too, suffers from the "divided consciousness," for the very language we use borrows from the male-dominant culture and helps to reproduce it, marring it "with inner inconsistencies and tensions."

> We have been led astray by terms that did not really fit women's situation. Women have been likened to slaves, to a caste, a class, a minority. Like all analogies, there were points of correspondence that did illuminate the situation of women—and points of divergence that were utterly obscured.

At the same time, feminist theory represents a transcendence, a turning of "alienation into a positive position, a chosen stance." Woman's social experience as outsider provides a different reality that can illuminate the social nature of her existence. The resulting awareness of the self as conditioned by a larger whole will provide an exit point from the "divided consciousness" and access to the "doubled vision," hence to a clearer commitment to the genuine liberation of women. As Kelly wrote:

> The step into feminist consciousness is a step beyond all the consciousness we bring with us, even at that marginal place on the boundary.   ·

Joan Kelly's work points a new direction for feminist theory. It emphasizes the centrality of consciousness. It insists on the importance of women's own experience, including that of resistance and struggle, in demystifying misogynist culture. It urges the use of sex and gender as analytic categories. The cumulative power of her work is measured by the extent to which her ideas have already been incorporated into history and theory; its continuing impact will be felt by the extent to which the ideas in this volume move us to action. Kelly expressed her own hopes for the impact of feminism on the future: "I want women to take the lead. . . . I know women will struggle for a social order of peace, equality, joy."

Blanche W. Cook, Clare Coss,
Alice K. Harris, Rosalind P. Petchesky,
and Amy Swerdlow

ONE

The Social Relation of the Sexes
Methodological Implications of Women's History

W omen's history has a dual goal: to restore women to history and to restore our history to women. In the past few years, it has stimulated a remarkable amount of research as well as a number of conferences and courses on the activities, status, and views of and about women. The interdisciplinary character of our concern with women has also newly enriched this vital historical work. But there is another aspect of women's history that needs to be considered: its theoretical significance, its implications for historical study in general.[1] In seeking to add women to the fund of historical knowledge, women's history has revitalized theory, for it has shaken the conceptual foundations of historical study. It has done this by making problematical three of the basic concerns of historical thought: (1) periodization, (2) the categories of social analysis, and (3) theories of social change.

Since all three issues are presently in ferment, I can at best suggest how they may be fruitfully posed. But in so doing, I should also like to show how the conception of these problems expresses a notion which is basic to feminist consciousness, namely, that the relation between the sexes is a social and not a natural one. This perception forms the core idea that upsets traditional thinking in all three cases.

Reprinted by permission from *Signs: Journal of Women in Culture and Society* 1, no. 4 (Summer 1976): 809–23.

1

Periodization

Once we look to history for an understanding of women's situation, we are, of course, already assuming that woman's situation is a social matter. But history, as we first came to it, did not seem to confirm this awareness. Throughout historical time, women have been largely excluded from making war, wealth, laws, governments, art, and science. Men, functioning in their capacity as historians, considered exactly those activities constitutive of civilization: hence, diplomatic history, economic history, constitutional history, and political and cultural history. Women figured chiefly as exceptions, those who were said to be as ruthless as, or wrote like, or had the brains of men. In redressing this neglect, women's history recognized from the start that what we call compensatory history is not enough. This was not to be a history of exceptional women, although they too need to be restored to their rightful places. Nor could it be another subgroup of historical thought, a history of women to place alongside the list of diplomatic history, economic history, and so forth, for all these developments impinged upon the history of women. Hence feminist scholarship in history, as in anthropology, came to focus primarily on the issue of women's status. I use "status" here and throughout in an expanded sense, to refer to woman's place and power—that is, the roles and positions women hold in society by comparison with those of men.

In historical terms, this means to look at ages or movements of great social change in terms of their liberation or repression of woman's potential, their import for the advancement of her humanity as well as "his." The moment this is done—the moment one assumes that women are a part of humanity in the fullest sense—the period or set of events with which we deal takes on a wholly different character or meaning from the normally accepted one. Indeed, what emerges is a fairly regular pattern of relative loss of status for women precisely in those periods of so-called progressive change. Since the dramatic new perspectives that unfold from this shift of vantage point have already been discussed at several conferences, I shall be brief here.[2] Let me merely point out that if we apply Fourier's famous dictum—that the emancipation of women is an index of the general emancipation of an age—our notions of so-called progressive developments, such as classical Athenian civilization, the Renaissance, and the French Revolution, undergo a startling re-evaluation. For women, "progress" in Athens meant concubinage and confinement of citizen wives in the gynecaeum. In Renaissance Europe it meant domestication of the bourgeois wife and escalation of witchcraft persecution which crossed class lines. And the Revolution expressly excluded women from its liberty, equality, and "fraternity." Suddenly we see these ages with a new double vision—and each eye sees a different picture.

Only one of these views has been represented by history up to now. Regardless of how these periods have been assessed, they have been assessed from the vantage point of men. Liberal historiography in particular, which considers all three periods as stages in the progressive realization of an individualistic social and cultural order, expressly maintains—albeit without considering the evidence—that women shared these advances with men. In Renaissance scholarship, for example, almost all historians have been content to situate women exactly where Jacob Burckhardt placed them in 1890: "on a footing of perfect equality with men." For a period that rejected the hierarchy of social class and the hierarchy of religious values in its restoration of a classical, secular culture, there was also, they claim, "no question of 'woman's rights' or female emancipation, simply because the thing itself was a matter of course."[3] Now while it is true that a couple of dozen women can be assimilated to the humanistic standard of culture which the Renaissance imposed upon itself, what is remarkable is that *only* a couple of dozen women can. To pursue this problem is to become aware of the fact that there was no "renaissance" for women—at least not during the Renaissance. There was, on the contrary, a marked restriction of the scope and powers of women. Moreover, this restriction is a consequence of the very developments for which the age is noted.[4]

What feminist historiography has done is to unsettle such accepted evaluations of historical periods. It has disabused us of the notion that the history of women is the same as the history of men, and that significant turning points in history have the same impact for one sex as for the other. Indeed, some historians now go so far as to maintain that, because of woman's particular connection with the function of reproduction, history could, and women's history should, be rewritten and periodized from this point of view, according to major turning points affecting childbirth, sexuality, family structure, and so forth.[5] In this regard, Juliet Mitchell refers to modern contraception as a "world-historic event"—although the logic of her thought, and my own, protests against a periodization that is primarily geared to changes in reproduction. Such criteria threaten to detach psychosexual development and family patterns from changes in the general social order, or to utterly reverse the causal sequence. Hence I see in them a potential isolation of women's history from what has hitherto been considered the mainstream of social change.

To my mind, what is more promising about the way periodization has begun to function in women's history is that it has become *relational*. It relates the history of women to that of men, as Engels did in *The Origin of the Family, Private Property and the State*, by seeing in common social developments institutional reasons for the advance of one sex and oppression of the other. Handled this way, traditional periodizing concepts may well be retained—and ought to be insofar as they refer to major structural changes in society. But in the evaluation of such changes we need to consider their effects upon women as distinct from men. We expect by now that those effects may be so different as to be opposed and that such opposition will be socially explicable. When women are excluded from the benefits of the economic, political, and cultural advances made in certain periods, a situation which gives women a different historical experience from men, it is to those "advances" we must look to find the reasons for that separation of the sexes.

Sex as a Social Category

Two convictions are implicit in this more complete and more complex sense of periodization: one, that women do form a distinctive social group and, second, that the invisibility of this group in traditional history is not to be ascribed to female nature. These notions, which clearly arise out of feminist consciousness, effect another, related change in the conceptual foundations of history by introducing sex as a category of social thought.

Feminism has made it evident that the mere fact of being a woman meant having a particular kind of social and hence historical experience, but the exact meaning of "woman" in this historical or social sense has not been so clear. What accounts for woman's situation as "other," and what perpetuates it historically? The "Redstockings Manifesto" of 1969 maintained that "women are an oppressed class" and suggested that the relations between men and women are class relations, that "sexual politics" are the politics of class domination. The most fruitful consequence of this conception of women as a social class has been the extension of class analysis to women by Marxist feminists such as Margaret Benston and Sheila Rowbotham.[6] They have traced the roots of woman's secondary status in history to economics inasmuch as women as a group have had a distinctive relation to production and property in almost all societies. The personal and psychological consequences of secondary status can be seen to flow from this special relation to work. As Rowbotham and Benston themselves make clear, however, it is one thing to extend the tools of class analysis to women and quite another to maintain that women *are* a class. Women belong to social classes, and the new women's history and histories of feminism have borne this out, demonstrating, for example, how class divisions disrupted and shattered the first wave of the feminist movement in nonsocialist countries, and how feminism has been expressly subordinated to the class struggle in socialist feminism.[7]

On the other hand, although women may adopt the interests and ideology of men of their class, women as a group cut through male class systems. Although I would quarrel with the notion that women of all classes, in all cultures, and at all times are accorded secondary status, there is certainly sufficient evidence that this is generally, if not universally, the case. From the advent of civilization, and hence of history proper as distinct from prehistorical societies, the social order has been patriarchal. Does that then make women a caste, a hereditary inferior order? This notion has its uses, too, as does the related one drawn chiefly from American black experience, which regards women as a minority group.[8] The sense of "otherness" which both these ideas convey is essential to our historical awareness of women as an oppressed social group. They help us appreciate the social formation of "femininity" as an internalization of ascribed inferiority which serves, at the same time, to manipulate those who have the authority women lack. As explanatory concepts, however, notions of caste and minority group are not productive when applied to women. *Why* should this majority be a minority? And why is it that the members of this particular caste, unlike all other castes, are not of the same rank throughout society? Clearly the minority psychology of women, like their caste status and qausi-class oppression, has to be traced to the universally distinguishing feature of all women, namely their sex. Any effort to understand women in terms of social categories that obscure this fundamental fact has to fail, only to make more appropriate concepts available. As Gerda Lerner put it, laying all such attempts to rest: "All analogies—class, minority group, caste—approximate the position of women, but fail to define it adequately. Women are a category unto themselves: an adequate analysis of their position in society demands new conceptual tools."[9] In short, women have to be defined as women. We are the social opposite, not of a class, a caste, or of a majority, since we are a majority, but of a sex: men. We are a sex, and categorization by gender no longer implies a mothering role and subordination to men, except as social role and relation recognized as such, as socially constructed and socially imposed.

A good part of the initial excitement in women's studies consisted of this discovery, that what had been taken as "natural" was in fact man-made, both as social order and as description of that order as natural and physically determined. Examples of such ideological reasoning go back to the story of Eve, but the social sciences have been functioning the same way, as myth reinforcing patriarchy. A feminist psychologist argues: "It is scientifically unacceptable to advocate the natural superiority of women as child-rearers and socializers of children when there have been so few studies of the effects of male-infant or father-infant interaction on the subsequent development of the child."[10] An anthropologist finds herself constrained to reject, and suspect, so-called scientific contentions that the monogamous family and male dominance belong to primates in general. In fact, she points out, "these features are *not* universal among non-human primates, including some of those most closely related to humans." And when male domination and male hierarchies do appear, they "seem to be adaptations to particular environments."[11]

Historians could not lay claim to special knowledge about the "natural" roles and relation of the sexes, but they knew what that order was, or ought to be. History simply tended to confirm it. *Bryan's Dictionary of Painters and Engravers* of 1904 says of the Renaissance artist, Propertia Rossi: "a lady of Bologna, best known as a sculptor and carver, but who also engraved upon copper, and learnt drawing and design from Marc Antonio. She is said to have been remarkable for her beauty, virtues, and talents, and to have died at an early age in 1530, in consequence of unrequited love. Her last work was a bas-relief of Joseph and Potiphar's wife!"[12] An exclamation mark ends the entry like a poke in the ribs, signifying that the "lady" (which is not a class designation here), who was beautiful and unhappy in love, was naturally absorbed by just that. Historians really *knew* why there were no great women artists. That is why it was not a historical problem until the feminist art historian, Linda Nochlin, posed it as such—by inquiring into the institutional factors, rather than the native gifts, that sustain artistic activity.[13]

When the issue of woman's place did appear openly, and male historians such as H. D. Kitto rose to defend "their" society, the Greek in his case, the natural order of things again came to the rescue.[14] If Athenian wives were not permitted to go about at will, weren't they too delicate for the strain that travel imposed in those days? If they played no role in political life—the activity that was the source of human dignity to the Greek—was it not because government covered "matters which, inescapably, only men could judge from their own experience and execute by their own exertions"? If girls were not being schooled, weren't they being instructed by mother in the arts of the female citizen? ("If we say 'housework,'" Kitto admits, "it sounds degrading, but if we say Domestic Science it sounds eminently respectable; and we have seen how varied and responsible it was.") But Kitto's major argument was reserved for the family: its religious and social importance in Athenian society. His reasoning on this point sounds to us like an incomplete sentence. He rightly points out that extinction of a family or dissipation of its property was regarded as a disaster. But for him, this fact is an argument, for his position is that it *is* woman's "natural" place to serve that family and continue it by raising legitimate heirs through whom to pass on its property and its rites. If under the conditions of Greek society that task should require confinement to the household and its rounds, that justifies the legal disabilities of wives. As for the other orders of women Athenian society demanded and regulated by law, concubines are not mentioned and hetaerae are "adventuresses who had said No to the serious business of life. Of course they amused men—'But, my dear fellow, one doesn't marry a woman like that.'"

Kitto wrote his history in 1951.

If our understanding of the Greek contribution to social life and consciousness now demands an adequate representation of the life experience of women, so too the sexual order, as shaped by the institutions of family and state, is a matter we now regard as not merely worthy of historical inquiry but central to it. This, I think, is a second major contribution women's history has made to the theory and practice of history in general. We have made of sex a category as fundamental to our analysis of the social order as other classifications, such as class and race. And we consider the relation of the sexes, as those of class and race, to be socially rather than naturally constituted, to have its own development, varying with changes in social organization. Embedded in and shaped by the social order, the relation of the sexes must be integral to any study of it. Our new sense of periodization reflects an assessment of historical change from the vantage point of women as well as men. Our use of sex as a social category means that our conception of historical change itself, as change in the social order, is broadened to include changes in the relation of the sexes.

I find the idea of the social relation of the sexes, which is at the core of this conceptual development, to be both novel and central in feminist scholarship and in works stimulated by it. An art historian, Carol Duncan, asks with respect to modern erotic art, "what are the male-female relations it implies," and finds those relations of domination and victimization becoming more pronounced precisely as women's claims for equality were winning recognition.[15] Michelle Zimbalist Rosaldo, coeditor of a collection of studies by feminist anthropologists, speaks of the need for anthropology to develop a theoretical context "within which the social relation of the sexes can be investigated and understood."[16] Indeed almost all the essays in this collective work are concerned with the structure of the sexual order—patriarchal, matrifocal, and otherwise—of the societies they treat. In art history, anthropology, sociology, and history, studies of the status of women necessarily tend to strengthen the social and relational character of the idea of sex. The activity, power, and cultural evaluation of women simply cannot be assessed except in relational terms: by comparison and contrast with the activity, power, and cultural evaluation of men, and in relation to the institutions and social developments that shape the sexual order. To conclude this point, let me quote Natalie Zemon Davis's address to the Second Berkshire Conference on the History of Women in October 1975:

It seems to me that we should be interested in the history of both women and men, that we should not be working only on the subjected sex any more than an historian of class can focus exclusively on peasants. Our goal is to understand the significance of the *sexes*, of gender groups in the historical past. Our goal is to discover the range in sex roles and in sexual symbolism in different societies and periods, to find out what meaning they had and how they functioned to maintain the social order or to promote its change.[17]

Theories of Social Change

If the relationship of the sexes is as necessary to an understanding of human history as the social relationship of classes, what now needs to be worked out are the connections between changes in class and sex relations.[18] For this task, I suggest that we consider significant changes in the respective roles of men and women in the light of fundamental changes in the mode of production. I am not here proposing a simple socioeconomic scheme. A theory of social change that incorporates the relation of the sexes has to consider how general changes in production affect and shape production in the family and, thereby, the respective roles of men and women. And it has to consider, as well, the flow in the other direction: the impact of family life and the relation of the sexes upon psychic and social formations.

The study of changes in the social relation of the sexes is new, even if we trace it as far back as Bachhofen, Morgan, and Engels. Engels in particular solidly established the social character of woman's relation to man, although it was only one change in that relation—albeit the major one—that concerned him: the transition to patriarchy with the advance from kin society to civilization, and the overthrow of patriarchy with the advent of socialism. His analysis of the subordination of women in terms of the emergence of private property and class inequality is basic to much of feminist scholarship today. Engels had almost no effect upon historical scholarship, except for socialist theorists such as August Bebel, and historians of women such as Emily James Putnam and Simone de Beauvoir, but contemporary efforts to understand the social causes of patriarchy, and the reasons for the various forms it takes, tend to confirm his ideas on the social relation of the sexes. Certain conclusions, which in turn open new directions for historical and anthropological research, can already be drawn from this recent work. One is that "woman's social position has not always, everywhere, or in most respects been subordinate to that of men."[19] I am quoting here from an anthropologist because the historical case for anything other than a patriarchal sexual order is considerably weaker. The dominant causal feature that emerges from anthropological studies of the sexual order (in the Rosaldo and Lamphere collection I have mentioned) is whether, and to what extent, the domestic and the public spheres of activity are separated from each other. Although what constitutes "domestic" and what "public" varies from culture to culture, and the lines of demarcation are differently drawn, a consistent pattern emerges when societies are placed on a scale where, at one end, familial and public activities are fairly merged, and, at the other, domestic and public activities are sharply differentiated.

Where familial activities coincide with public or social ones, the status of women is comparable or even superior to that of men. This pattern is very much in agreement with Engels's ideas, because in such situations the means of subsistence and production are commonly held and a communal household is the focal point of both domestic and social life. Hence it is so- cieties where production for exchange is slight and where pri- vate property and class inequality are not developed that sex in- equalities are least evident. Women's roles are as varied as men's, although there are sex-role differences; authority and power are shared by women and men rather than vested in a hierarchy of males; women are highly evaluated by the culture; and women and men have comparable sexual rights.

The most one can say about the sexual division of labor in so- cieties at this end of the scale is that there is a tendency toward mother/child or women/children grouping and toward male hunting and warfare. This "natural" division of labor, if such it is, is not yet socially determined. That is, men as well as women care for children and perform household tasks, and women as well as men hunt. The social organization of work, and the ritu- als and values that grow out of it, do not serve to separate out the sexes and place one under the authority of the other. They do just that at the opposite end of the scale where the domestic and public orders are clearly distinguished from each other. Women continue to be active producers all the way up the scale (and must continue to be so until there is considerable wealth and class inequality), but they steadily lose control over prop- erty, products, and themselves as surplus increases, private property develops, and the communal household becomes a private economic unit, a family (extended or nuclear) repre- sented by a man. The family itself, the sphere of women's activi- ties, is in turn subordinated to a broader social or public order— governed by a state—which tends to be the domain of men. This is the general pattern presented by historical or civilized societies.[20]

As we move in this direction on the scale, it becomes evident that sexual inequalities are bound to the control of property. It is interesting to note in this regard that in several societies class inequalities are expressed in sexual terms. Women who have property, in livestock, for example, may use it for bridewealth to purchase "wives" who serve them.[21] This example, which seems to confound sex and class, actually indicates how sex and class relations differ. Although property establishes a class inequality among such women, it is nevertheless "wives," that is, women as a group, who constitute a propertyless serving order attached to a domestic kind of work, including horticulture.

How does this attachment of women to domestic work develop, and what forms does it take? This process is one of the central problems confronting feminist anthropology and history. By definition, this query rejects the traditional, simple biological "reasons" for the definition of woman-as-domestic. The privatizing of child rearing and domestic work and the sex typing of that work are social, not natural, matters. I suggest, therefore, that in treating this problem, we continue to look at *property relations* as the basic determinant of the sexual division of labor and of the sexual order. The more the domestic and the public domains are differentiated, the more work, and hence property, are of two clearly distinguishable kinds. There is production for subsistence and production for exchange. However the productive system of a society is organized, it operates, as Marx pointed out, as a continuous process which reproduces itself: that is, its material means and instruments, its people, and the social relations among them. Looked at as a continuous process (what Marx meant by reproduction), the productive work of society thus includes procreation and the socialization of children who must find their places within the social order.[22] I suggest that what shapes the relation of the sexes is the way this work of procreation and socialization is organized in relation to the organization of work that results in articles for subsistence and/or exchange. In sum, what patriarchy means as a general social order is that women function as the property of men in the maintenance and production of new members of the social order; that these relations of production are worked out in the organization of kin and family; and that other forms of work, such as production of goods and services for immediate use, are generally, although not always, attached to these procreative and socializing functions.[23]

Inequalities of sex as well as class are traced to property relations and forms of work in this scheme, but there are certain evident differences between the two. In the public domain, by which I mean the social order that springs from the organization of the general wealth and labor of society, class inequalities are paramount. For the relation of the sexes, control or lack of control of the property that separates people into owners and workers is not significant. What *is* significant is whether women *of either class* have equal relations to work or property with men of their class.

In the household or family, on the other hand, where ownership of all property resides in historic societies characterized by private property, sex inequalities are paramount and they cut through class lines. What is significant for the domestic relation is that women in the family, like serfs in feudal Europe, can both have and *be* property. To quote from an ancient description of early Roman law,

> a woman joined to her husband by a holy marriage, should share in all his possessions and sacred rites. . . . This law obliged both the married women, as having no other refuge, to conform themselves entirely to the temper of their husbands and the husbands to rule their wives as necessary and inseparable possessions. Accordingly, if a wife was virtuous and in all things obedient to her husband, she was mistress of the house to the same degree as her husband was master of it, and after the death of her husband she was heir to his property in the same manner as a daughter. . . . But if she did any wrong, the injured party was her judge, and determined the degree of her punishment. . . .[24]

Regardless of class, and regardless of ownership (although these modify the situation in interesting ways), women have generally functioned as the property of men in the procreative and socializing aspect of the productive work of their society. Women constitute part of the means of production of the private family's mode of work.

Patriarchy, in short, is at home at home. The private family is its proper domain. But the historic forms that patriarchy takes, like its very origin, are to be traced to the society's mode of production. The sexual order varies with the general organization of property and work because this shapes both family and public domains and determines how they approach or recede from each other.

These relations between the domestic and the public orders,

in turn, account for many of the unexpected oppositions and juxtapositions expressed by our new sense of historical periods.[25] Blurring the lines between family and society diminished a number of sexual inequalities, including the double standard, for feudal noblewomen, for example, as well as for women in advanced capitalistic societies. The status of the feudal noblewoman was high before the rise of the state when the family order *was* the public order of her class; and the scope that familial political power gave women included the Church where aristocratic women also commanded a sphere of their own. Again today, the two domains approach each other as private household functions—child rearing, production of food and clothing, nursing, and so forth—become socially organized. Women can again work and associate with each other outside the household, and the sexual division of labor, although far from overcome, appears increasingly irrational.

Where domestic and public realms pulled apart, however, sexual inequalities became pronounced as did the simultaneous demand for female chastity and prostitution. This was the case with Athens of the classical period, where the private household economy was the basic form of production and the social or public order of the polis consisted of many such households which were subordinate to and governed by it. Wives of the citizenry were confined to the order of the household: to production of legitimate heirs and supervision of indoor slave production of goods and services for use. Although necessary to the public order, wives did not directly belong to or participate in it, and free women who fell outside the domestic order and its property arrangements fell outside the public order as well. The situation of women was much the same in the middle classes of modern Europe, although here capitalist commodity production moved out of the home and became socially organized. What capitalist production did was to turn the working-class family, too, after an initial, almost disastrous onslaught upon it, into a complement of social production. The family in modern society has served as the domain for the production and training of the working class. It has been the alleged reason for women having to function as underpaid, irregular laborers whose wages generally had to be supplemented by sexual attachment to a man, inside or outside family arrangements. And it has served to compensate the worker whose means of subsistence were alienated from him but who could have private property in his wife.

Such has been the institutionally determined role of the family under capitalism, and women of both the owning and the working classes, women both in and outside the family, have had their outer and inner lives shaped by the structure of its social relations.

Surely a dominant reason for studying the social relation of the sexes is political. To understand the interests, aside from the personal interests of individual men, that are served by the retention of an unequal sexual order is in itself liberating. It detaches an age-old injustice from the blind operation of social forces and places it in the realm of choice. This is why we look to the organization of the productive forces of society to understand the shape and structure of the domestic order to which women have been primarily attached.

But women's history also opens up the other half of history, viewing women as agents and the family as a productive and social force. The most novel and exciting task of the study of the social relation of the sexes is still before us: to appreciate how we are all, women and men, initially humanized, turned into social creatures by the work of that domestic order to which women have been primarily attached. Its character and the structure of its relations order our consciousness, and it is through this consciousness that we first view and construe our world.[26] To understand the historical impact of women, family, and the relation of the sexes upon society serves a less evident political end, but perhaps a more strictly feminist one. For if the historical conception of civilization can be shown to include the psychosocial functions of the family, then with that understanding we can insist that any reconstruction of society along just lines incorporate reconstruction of the family—all kinds of collective and private families, and all of them functioning, not as property relations, but as personal relations among freely associating people.

Notes

1. The central theme of this paper emerged from regular group discussions, from which I have benefited so much, with Marilyn Arthur, Blanche Cook, Pamela Farley, Mary Feldblum, Alice Kessler-Harris, Amy Swerdlow, and Carole Turbin. Many of the ideas were sharpened in talks with Gerda Lerner, Renate

Bridenthal, Dick Vann, and Marilyn Arthur, with whom I served on several panels on women's history and its theoretical implications. My City College students in Marxism/feminism and in fear of women, witchcraft, and the family have stimulated my interests and enriched my understanding of many of the issues presented here. To Martin Fleisher and Nancy Miller I am indebted for valuable suggestions for improving an earlier version of this paper, which I delivered at the Barnard College Conference on the Scholar and the Feminist II: Toward New Criteria of Relevance, April 12, 1975.

2. Conference of New England Association of Women Historians, Yale University (October 1973): Marilyn Arthur, Renate Bridenthal, Joan Kelly-Gadol; Second Berkshire Conference on the History of Women, Radcliffe (October 1974): panel on "The Effects of Women's History upon Traditional Historiography," Renate Bridenthal, Joan Kelly-Gadol, Gerda Lerner, Richard Vann (papers deposited at Schlesinger Library); Sarah Lawrence symposium (March 1975): Marilyn Arthur, Renate Bridenthal, Gerda Lerner, Joan Kelly-Gadol (papers available as *Conceptual Frameworks in Women's History* [Bronxville, N.Y.: Sarah Lawrence Publications, 1976]). For some recent comments along some of these same lines, see Carl N. Degler, *Is There a History of Women?* (Oxford: Clarendon Press, 1975). As I edit this paper for printing, the present economic crisis is threatening the advances of feminist scholarship once again by forcing the recently arrived women educators out of their teaching positions and severing thereby the professional connections necessary to research and theory, such as the conferences mentioned above.

3. *The Civilization of the Renaissance in Italy* (London: Phaidon Press, 1950), p. 241. With the exception of Ruth Kelso, *Doctrine for the Lady of the Renaissance* (Urbana: University of Illinois Press, 1956), this view is shared by every work I know of on Renaissance women except for contemporary feminist historians. Even Simone de Beauvoir, and of course Mary Beard, regard the Renaissance as advancing the condition of women, although Burckhardt himself pointed out that the women of whom he wrote "had no thought of the public; their function was to influence distinguished men, and to moderate male impulse and caprice."

4. See the several contemporary studies recently or soon to be published on Renaissance women: Susan Bell, "Christine de Pizan," *Feminist Studies* (Winter 1975/1976); Joan Kelly-Gadol, "Notes on Women in the Renaissance and Renaissance Historiography," in *Conceptual Frameworks in Women's History* (n. 2 above); Margaret Leah King, "The Religious Retreat of Isotta Nogarola, 1418–66," *Signs* 3, no. 4 (Summer 1978): 807–22; an article on women in the Renaissance by Kathleen Casey in *Liberating Women's History*, Berenice Carroll, ed. (Urbana: University of Illinois Press, 1976); Joan Kelly-Gadol, "Did Women Have a Renaissance?" chap. 2.

5. Vann (n. 2 above).

6. "Redstockings Manifesto," in *Sisterhood Is Powerful*, ed. Robin Morgan (New York: Random House, 1970), pp. 533–36. Margaret Benston, *The Political Economy of Women's Liberation* (New York: Monthly Review, reprint, 1970). Sheila Rowbotham, *Woman's Consciousness, Man's World* (Middlesex: Pelican Books, 1973), with bibliography of the periodical literature. A number of significant articles applying Marxist analysis to the oppression of women have been appearing in issues of *Radical American* and *New Left Review*.

7. Eleanor Flexner, *Century of Struggle* (New York: Atheneum Publishers, 1970); Sheila Rowbotham, *Women, Resistance and Revolution* (New York: Random House, 1974); panel at the Second Berkshire Conference on the History of Women, Radcliffe (n. 2 above), on "Clara Zetkin and Adelheid Popp: The Development of Feminist Awareness in the Socialist Women's Movement—Germany and Austria, 1890–1914," with Karen Honeycutt, Ingurn LaFleur, and Jean Quataert. Karen Honeycutt's paper on Clara Zetkin is in *Feminist Studies* (Winter 1975/76).

8. Helen Mayer Hacker did interesting work along these lines in the 1950s, "Women as a Minority Group," *Social Forces* 30 (October 1951–May 1952): 60–69, and subsequently, "Women as a Minority Group: Twenty Years Later" (Pittsburgh: Know, Inc., 1972). Degler has recently taken up these classifications and also finds he must reject them (see n. 2 above).

9. "The Feminists: A Second Look," *Columbia Forum* 13 (Fall 1970): 24–30.

10. Rochelle Paul Wortis, "The Acceptance of the Concept of Maternal Role by Behavioral Scientists: Its Effects on Women," *American Journal of Orthopsychiatry* 41 (October 1971): 733–46.

11. Kathleen Gough, "The Origin of the Family," *Journal of Marriage and the Family* 33 (November 1971): 760–71.

12. London: Geo. Bell, 1904, 4:285.

13. "Why Have There Been No Great Women Artists?" *Art News* 69, no. 9 (January 1971): 22–39, 67–71.

14. *The Greeks* (Baltimore: Penguin Books, 1962), pp. 219–36.

15. "The Esthetics of Power" (unpublished). See also Carol Duncan, "Virility and Domination in Early 20th Century Vanguard Painting," *Artforum* 12 (December 1973): 30–39.

16. *Women, Culture and Society*, ed. Michelle Zimbalist Rosaldo and Louise Lamphere (Stanford, Calif.: Stanford University Press, 1974), p. 17.

17. Natalie Zemon Davis, "'Women's History' in Transition: The European Case," *Feminist Studies* 3, no. 3/4 (Winter 1975/76): 90.

18. See panel papers, *Conceptual Frameworks in Women's History* (n. 2 above).

19. Karen Sacks, "Engles Revisited," in Rosaldo and Lamphere, p. 207. See also Eleanor Leacock's introduction to Engels, *The Origin of the Family, Private Property and the State* (New York: International Publishers, 1972); also Leacock's paper delivered at Columbia University Seminar on Women in Society, April 1975.

20. On this point, one would like to see many more specific studies, as in n. 19 above, which trace in detail the process of social change that fosters male control of the new means of production for exchange, and with the new wealth, control of the broader social or public order and of the family as well. Historical studies of civilized societies would be useful for examples of extended processes of social change, including those of our own society.

21. E.g., among the Ibo, Mbuti, and Lovedu (see Rosaldo and Lamphere, pp. 149, 216).

22. In *Woman's Estate* (New York: Random House, 1973,) Juliet Mitchell (developing an earlier essay) offered the categories of reproduction/production within which to consider the history of women. This is roughly equivalent to the domestic/public categorization, except that she added sexuality and socialization as two further socially ordered functions which need not be attached to reproduc-

tion universally, although they have been under capitalism. I believe we must consider sexuality and socialization in any study of the sexual order: what are the relations among love, sex, and marriage in any society, for women and for men, heterosexual and homosexual, and who socializes which groups of children, by sex and by age, so that they find their places in the social order—including their sexual places. I also believe, as Juliet Mitchell does, that the evidence clearly warrants working out relations between the dominant mode of production in a society and the forms of reproduction, sexuality, and socialization. However, certain difficulties emerge, not in using this scheme so much as in using its terms—especially when we deal with precapitalist societies. Neither cultural nor political activities have a clearly definable place under the heading of production, as they do, e.g., when we use the terms domestic/public or, more simply, family and society. Another reason I prefer family/society or domestic/public, is that the terms production/reproduction tend to confound biological reproduction with social reproduction, and this obscures the essentially *productive* work of the family and the property relation between husband and wife. See my review of Rowbotham in *Science and Society* 39, no. 4 (Winter 1975/76): 471–74, and Lise Vogel's review essay on Juliet Mitchell, "The Earthly Family," *Radical America* 7 (Fall 1973): 9–50.

23. Ideas along these lines have been developed by Rowbotham, *Women's Consciousness, Man's World*; Bridget O'Laughlin, "Mediation of Contradiction: Why Mbum Women Do Not Eat Chicken," in Rosaldo and Lamphere, pp. 301–20.

24. Dionysius of Halicarnassus, *The Roman Antiquities*, trans. E. Cary (Cambridge, Mass.: Harvard University Press), 1: 381–82. Milton extended the property relationship between husband and wife to the Garden of Eden where Adam's possession of Eve constitutes the first example of private property: "Hail, wedded Love, mysterious law, true source/Of human offspring, sole propriety/In Paradise of all things common else!" (*Paradise Lost*, pt. 4, lines 750–51). Needless to say, where Eve serves Adam while he serves God, the "propriety" is not a mutual relation.

25. For the examples given here, see the articles on the periods in question in Bridenthal and Koonz (n. 4 above).

26. This is one of Rowbotham's points in *Woman's Consciousness, Man's World*. I believe it should lead to development of the genre of psychohistorical studies and studies in family history exemplified by Philippe Ariès, *Centuries of Childhood: A Social History of Family Life* (New York: Alfred A. Knopf, 1965); Nancy Chodorow, "Family Structure and Feminine Personality," in Rosaldo and Lamphere (n. 16), pp. 43–67; David Hunt, *Parents and Children in History* (New York: Harper & Row, 1972); the Frankfurt school in *Autorität und Familie*, ed. Max Horkheimer (Paris: Alcan, 1936): Wilhelm Reich, *The Mass Psychology of Fascism* (New York: Farrar, Straus & Giroux, 1970); and Eli Zaretsky, "Capitalism, the Family and Personal Life," *Socialist Revolution* nos. 13, 14, 16 (1973). See the excellent article on this mode of historical inquiry by Lawrence Stone, in the *New York Review of Books* 21 (November 14, 1974): 25.

TWO

Did Women Have a Renaissance?

O ne of the tasks of women's history is to call into question accepted schemes of periodization. To take the emancipation of women as a vantage point is to discover that events that further the historical development of men, liberating them from natural, social, or ideological constraints, have quite different, even opposite, effects upon women. The Renaissance is a good case in point. Italy was well in advance of the rest of Europe from roughly 1350 to 1530 because of its early consolidation of genuine states, the mercantile and manufacturing economy that supported them, and its working out of postfeudal and even postguild social relations. These developments reorganized Italian society along modern lines and opened the possibilities for the social and cultural expression for which the age is known. Yet precisely these developments affected women adversely, so much so that there was no renaissance for women— at least, not during the Renaissance. The state, early

Reprinted from *Becoming Visible: Women in European History*, edited by Renate Bridenthal and Claudia Koonz, © 1977 by Houghton Mifflin Co. Used by permission.

I first worked out these ideas in 1972–1973 in a course at Sarah Lawrence College entitled "Women: Myth and Reality" and am very much indebted to students in that course and my colleagues Eva Kollisch, Gerda Lerner, and Sherry Ortner. I thank Eve Fleisher, Martin Fleisher, Renate Bridenthal, and Claudia Koonz for their valuable criticism of an earlier version of this paper.

capitalism, and the social relations formed by them impinged on the lives of Renaissance women in different ways according to their different positions in society. But the startling fact is that women as a group, especially among the classes that dominated Italian urban life, experienced a contraction of social and personal options that men of their classes either did not, as was the case with the bourgeoisie, or did not experience as markedly, as was the case with the nobility.

Before demonstrating this point, which contradicts the widely held notion of the equality of Renaissance women with men,[1] we need to consider how to establish, let alone measure, loss or gain with respect to the liberty of women. I found the following criteria most useful for gauging the relative contraction (or expansion) of the powers of Renaissance women and for determining the quality of their historical experience: 1) the regulation of *female sexuality* as compared with male sexuality; 2) women's *economic* and *political roles*, i.e., the kind of work they performed as compared with men, and their access to property, political power, and the education or training necessary for work, property, and power; 3) the *cultural roles* of women in shaping the outlook of their society, and access to the education and/or institutions necessary for this; 4) *ideology* about women, in particular the sex-role system displayed or advocated in the symbolic products of the society, its art, literature, and philosophy. Two points should be made about this ideological index. One is its rich inferential value. The literature, art, and philosophy of a society, which give us direct knowledge of the attitudes of the dominant sector of that society toward women, also yield indirect knowledge about our other criteria: namely, the sexual, economic, political, and cultural activities of women. Insofar as images of women relate to what really goes on, we can infer from them something about that social reality. But, second, the relations between the ideology of sex roles and the reality we want to get at are complex and difficult to establish. Such views may be prescriptive rather than descriptive; they may describe a situation that no longer prevails; or they may use the relation of the sexes symbolically and not refer primarily to women and sex roles at all. Hence, to assess the historical significance of changes in sex-role conception, we must bring such changes

into connection with all we know about general developments
in the society at large.

This essay examines changes in sex-role conception, particularly with respect to sexuality, for what they tell us about Renaissance society and women's place in it. At first glance, Renaissance thought presents a problem in this regard because it cannot
be simply categorized. Ideas about the relation of the sexes
range from a relatively complementary sense of sex roles in literature dealing with courtly manners, love, and education, to patriarchal conceptions in writings on marriage and the family, to
a fairly equal presentation of sex roles in early Utopian social
theory. Such diversity need not baffle the attempt to reconstruct
a history of sex-role conceptions, however, and to relate its
course to the actual situation of women. Toward this end, one
needs to sort out this material in terms of the social groups to
which it responds: to courtly society in the first case, the nobility
of the petty despotic states of Italy; to the patrician bourgeoisie
in the second, particularly of republics such as Florence. In the
third case, the relatively equal position accorded women in Utopian thought (and in those lower-class movements of the radical
Reformation analogous to it) results from a larger critique of
early modern society and all the relations of domination that
flow from private ownership and control of property. Once distinguished, each of these groups of sources tells the same story.
Each discloses in its own way certain new constraints suffered
by Renaissance women as the family and political life were re-
structured in the great transition from medieval feudal society to
the early modern state. The sources that represent the interests
of the nobility and the bourgeoisie point to this fact by a telling,
double index. Almost all such works—with certain notable exceptions, such as Boccaccio and Ariosto—establish chastity as
the female norm and restructure the relation of the sexes to one
of female dependency and male domination.

The bourgeois writings on education, domestic life, and society constitute the extreme in this denial of women's independence. Suffice it to say that they sharply distinguish an inferior
domestic realm of women from the superior public realm of
men, achieving a veritable "renaissance" of the outlook and
practices of classical Athens, with its domestic imprisonment of

citizen wives.[2] The courtly Renaissance literature we will consider was more gracious. But even here, by analyzing a few of
the representative works of this genre, we find a new repression
of the noblewoman's affective experience, in contrast to the lati-
tude afforded her by medieval literature, and some of the social
and cultural reasons for it. Dante and Castiglione, who continued a literary tradition that began with the courtly love literature of eleventh- and twelfth-century Provence, transformed
medieval conceptions of love and nobility. In the love ideal they
formed, we can discern the inferior position the Renaissance noblewoman held in the relation of the sexes by comparison with
her male counterpart and with her medieval predecessor as well.

Love and the Medieval Lady

Medieval courtly love, closely bound to the dominant values
of feudalism and the church, allowed in a special way for the
expression of sexual love by women. Of course, only aristocratic
women gained their sexual and affective rights thereby. If a
knight wanted a peasant girl, the twelfth-century theorist of *The
Art of Courtly Love*, Andreas Capellanus, encouraged him "not
[to] hesitate to take what you seek and to embrace her by force."[3]
Toward the lady, however, "a true lover considers nothing good
except what he thinks will please his beloved"; for if courtly love
were to define itself as a noble phenomenon, it had to attribute
an essential freedom to the relation between lovers. Hence, it
metaphorically extended the social relation of vassalage to the
love relationship, a "conceit" that Maurice Valency rightly called
"the shaping principle of the whole design" of courtly love.[4]

Of the two dominant sets of dependent social relations formed
by feudalism—*les liens de dépendence*, as Marc Bloch called them
—vassalage, the military relation of knight to lord, distinguished
itself (in its early days) by being freely entered into. At a time
when everyone was somebody's "man," the right to freely enter
a relation of service characterized aristocratic bonds, whereas
hereditability marked the servile work relation of serf to lord.
Thus, in medieval romances, a parley typically followed a declaration of love until love freely proffered was freely returned.
A kiss (like the kiss of homage) sealed the pledge, rings were
exchanged, and the knight entered the love service of his lady.

Representing love along the lines of vassalage had several liberating implications for aristocratic women. Most fundamental, ideas of homage and mutuality entered the notion of heterosexual relations along with the idea of freedom. As symbolized on shields and other illustrations that place the knight in the ritual attitude of commendation, kneeling before his lady with his hands folded between hers, homage signified male service, not domination or subordination of the lady, and it signified fidelity, constancy in that service. "A lady must honor her lover as a friend, not as a master," wrote Marie de Ventadour, a female troubadour or *trobairitz*.[5] At the same time, homage entailed a reciprocity of rights and obligations, a service on the lady's part as well. In one of Marie de France's romances, a knight is about to be judged by the barons of King Arthur's court when his lady rides to the castle to give him "succor" and pleads successfully for him, as any overlord might.[6] Mutuality, or complementarity, marks the relation the lady entered into with her *ami* (the favored name for "lover" and, significantly, a synonym for "vassal").

This relation between knight and lady was very much at variance with the patriarchal family relations obtaining in that same level of society. Aware of its incompatibility with prevailing family and marital relations, the celebrants of courtly love kept love detached from marriage. "We dare not oppose the opinion of the Countess of Champagne who rules that love can exert no power between husband and wife," Andreas wrote (p. 175). But in opting for a free and reciprocal heterosexual relation outside marriage, the poets and theorists of courtly love ignored the almost universal demand of patriarchal society for female chastity, in the sense of the woman's strict bondage to the marital bed. The reasons why they did so, and even the fact that they did so, have long been disputed, but the ideas and values that justify this kind of adulterous love are plain. Marriage, as a relation arranged by others, carried the taint of social necessity for the aristocracy. And if the feudality denigrated marriage by disdaining obligatory service, the church did so by regarding it not as a "religious" state, but an inferior one that responded to natural necessity. Moreover, Christianity positively fostered the ideal of courtly love at a deep level of feeling. The courtly relation between lovers took vassalage as its structural model, but its passion was nourished by Christianity's exaltation of love.

Christianity had accomplished its elevation of love by purging it of sexuality, and in this respect, by recombining the two, courtly love clearly departed from Christian teaching. The toleration of adultery it fostered thereby was in itself not so grievous. The feudality disregarded any number of church rulings that affected their interests, such as prohibitions of tournaments and repudiation of spouses (divorce) and remarriage. Moreover, adultery hardly needed the sanction of courtly love, which, if anything, acted rather as a restraining force by binding sexuality (except in marriage) to love. Lancelot, in Chrétien de Troyes's twelfth-century romance, lies in bed with a lovely woman because of a promise he has made, but "not once does he look at her, nor show her any courtesy. Why not? Because his heart does not go out to her. . . . The knight has only one heart, and this one is no longer really his, but has been entrusted to someone else, so that he cannot bestow it elsewhere."[7] Actually, Lancelot's chastity represented more of a threat to Christian doctrine than the fact that his passion (for Guinevere) was adulterous, because his attitudes justified sexual love. Sexuality could only be "mere sexuality" for the medieval church, to be consecrated and directed toward procreation by Christian marriage. Love, on the other hand, defined as passion for the good, perfects the individual; hence love, according to Thomas Aquinas, properly directs itself toward God.[8] Like the churchman, Lancelot spurned mere sexuality—but for the sake of sexual love. He defied Christian *teaching* by reattaching love to sex; and experiencing his love as a devout vocation, as a passion, he found himself in utter accord with Christian *feeling*. His love, as Chrétien's story makes clear, is sacramental as well as sexual:

> . . . then he comes to the bed of the Queen, whom he adores and before whom he kneels, holding her more dear than the relic of any saint. And the Queen extends her arms to him and, embracing him, presses him tightly against her bosom, drawing him into the bed beside her and showing him every possible satisfaction. . . . Now Lancelot possesses all he wants. . . . It cost him such pain to leave her that he suffered a real martyr's agony. . . . When he leaves the room, he bows and acts precisely as if he were before a shrine. (p. 329)

It is difficult to assess Christianity's role in this acceptance of feeling and this attentiveness to inner states that characterize medieval lyric and romance, although the weeping and wringing of hands, the inner troubles and turmoil of the love genre, were to disappear with the restoration of classical attitudes of restraint in the Renaissance. What certainly bound courtly love to Christianity, however, aside from its positive attitude toward feeling, was the cultivation of decidedly "romantic" states of feeling. In Christian Europe, *passion* acquired a positive, spiritual meaning that classical ethics and classical erotic feeling alike denied it. Religious love and courtly love were both suffered as a destiny, were both submitted to and not denied. Converted by a passion that henceforth directed and dominated them and for which all manner of suffering could be borne, the courtly lovers, like the religious, sought a higher emotional state than ordinary life provided. They sought ecstasy; and this required of them a heroic discipline, an ascetic fortitude, and single-mindedness. Love and its ordeals alike removed them from the daily, the customary, the routine, setting them apart as an elite superior to the conventions of marriage and society.

Religious feeling and feudal values thus both fed into a conception of passionate love that, because of its mutuality, required that women, too, partake of that passion, of that adulterous sexual love. The lady of medieval romance also suffered. She suffered "more pain for love than ever a woman suffered" in another of Marie de France's romances. As the jealously guarded wife of an old man, ravished by the beauty of her knight when she first saw him, she could not rest for love of him, and *"franc et noble"* (i.e., free) as she was, she granted him her kiss and her love upon the declaration of his—"and many other caresses which lovers know well" during the time she hid him in her castle.[9] So common is this sexual mutuality to the literature of courtly love that one cannot take seriously the view of it as a form of Madonna worship in which a remote and virginal lady spurns consummation. That stage came later, as courtly love underwent its late medieval and Renaissance transformation. But for the twelfth century, typical concerns of Provençal *iocs-partitz*, those poetic "questions" on love posed at court (and reflecting the social reality of mock courts of love played out as a diversion) were: "Must a lady do for her lover as much as he for her?"; or, "A husband learns that his wife has a lover. The wife and the lover perceive it—which of the three is in the greatest strait?"[10] In the same vein, Andreas Capellanus perceived differences between so-called "pure" and "mixed" love as accidental, not substantial. Both came from the same feeling of the heart and one could readily turn into the other, as circumstances dictated. Adultery, after all, required certain precautions; but that did not alter the essentially erotic nature even of "pure" love, which went "as far as the kiss and the embrace and the modest contact with the nude lover, omitting the final solace" (p. 122).

The sexual nature of courtly love, considered together with its voluntary character and the nonpatriarchal structure of its relations, makes us question what it signifies for the actual condition of feudal women. For clearly it represents an ideological liberation of their sexual and affective powers that must have some social reference. This is not to raise the fruitless question of whether such love relationships actually existed or if they were mere literary conventions. The real issue regarding ideology is, rather, what kind of society could posit *as a social ideal* a love relation outside of marriage, one that women freely entered and that, despite its reciprocity, made women the gift givers while men did the service. What were the social conditions that fostered these particular conventions rather than the more common ones of female chastity and/or dependence?

No one doubts that courtly love spread widely as a convention. All ranks and both sexes of the aristocracy wrote troubadour poetry and courtly romances and heard them sung and recited in courtly gatherings throughout most of medieval Europe. But this could happen only if such ideas supported the male-dominated social order rather than subverted it. The love motif could, and with Gottfried of Strasbourg's *Tristan* (c. 1210) did, stand as an ideal radically opposed to the institutions of the church and emerging feudal kingship. But in its beginnings, and generally, courtly love no more threatened Christian feeling or feudalism than did chivalry, which brought a certain "sacramental" moral value and restraint to the profession of warfare. While courtly love celebrated sexuality, it enriched and deepened it by means of the Christian notion of passion. While the knight often betrayed his lord to serve his lord's lady, he transferred to that relationship the feudal ideal of freely committed, mutual service. And while passionate love led to adultery, by that very fact it reinforced, as its necessary premise, the practice of political marriage. The literature of courtly love suppressed rather than exaggerated tensions between it and other social values, and the reason for this lies deeper than literature. It lies at the institutional level, where there was real agreement, or at least no contradiction, between the sexual and affective needs of women and the interests of the aristocratic family, which the feudality and church alike regarded as fundamental to the social order.

The factors to consider here are property and power on the one hand, and illegitimacy on the other. Feudalism, as a system of private jurisdictions, bound power to landed property; and it permitted both inheritance and administration of feudal property by women.[11] Inheritance by women often suited the needs of the great landholding families, as their unremitting efforts to secure such rights for their female members attest. The authority of feudal women owes little to any gallantry on the part of feudal society. But the fact that women could hold both ordinary fiefs and vast collections of counties—and exercise in their own right the seigniorial powers that went with them—certainly fostered a gallant attitude. Eleanor of Aquitaine's adultery as wife of the king of France could have had dire consequences in another place at another time, say in the England of Henry VIII. In her case, she moved on to a new marriage with the future Henry II of England or, to be more exact, a new alliance connecting his Plantagenet interests with her vast domains centering on Provence. Women also exercised power during the absence of warrior husbands. The lady presided over the court at such times, administered the estates, took charge of the vassal services due the lord. She *was* the lord—albeit in his name rather than her own—unless widowed and without male children. In the religious realm, abbesses exercised analogous temporal as well as spiritual jurisdiction over great territories, and always in their own right, in virtue of their office.

This social reality accounts for the retention of matronymics in medieval society, that is, a common use of the maternal name, which reflects the position of women as landowners and managers of great estates, particularly during the crusading period.[12] It also accounts for the husband's toleration of his wife's diversions, if discreetly pursued. His primary aim to get and maintain a fief required her support, perhaps even her inheritance. As

Emily James Putnam put it, "It would, perhaps, be paradoxical to say that a baron would prefer to be sure that his tenure was secure than that his son was legitimate, but it is certain that the relative value of the two things had shifted."[13] Courtly literature, indeed, reveals a marked lack of concern about illegitimacy. Although the ladies of the romances are almost all married, they seldom appear with children, let alone appear to have their lives and loves complicated by them. Much as the tenet that love thrives only in adultery reflected and reinforced the stability of arranged marriage, so the political role of women, and the indivisibility of the fief, probably underlies this indifference to illegitimacy. Especially as forms of inheritance favoring the eldest son took hold in the course of the twelfth century to preserve the great houses, the claims of younger sons and daughters posed no threat to family estates. Moreover, the expansive, exploitative aristocratic families of the eleventh and twelfth centuries could well afford illegitimate members. For the feudality, they were no drain as kin but rather a source of strength in marital alliances and as warriors.

For all these reasons, feudal Christian society could promote the ideal of courtly love. We could probably maintain of any ideology that tolerates sexual parity that: 1) it can threaten no major institution of the patriarchal society from which it emerges; and 2) men, the rulers within the ruling order, must benefit by it. Courtly love surely fit these requirements. That such an ideology did actually develop, however, is due to another feature of medieval society, namely, the cultural activity of feudal women. For responsive as courtly love might seem to men of the feudality whose erotic needs it objectified and refined, as well as objectifying their consciousness of the social self (as noble), it did this and more for women. It gave women lovers, peers rather than masters; and it gave them a justifying ideology for adultery which, as the more customary double standard indicates, men in patriarchal society seldom require. Hence, we should expect what we indeed find: women actively shaping these ideas and values that corresponded so well to their particular interests.

In the first place, women participated in creating the literature of courtly love, a major literature of their era. This role they had not been able to assume in the culture of classical Greece or

Rome. The notable exception of Sappho only proves the point: it took women to give poetic voice and status to female sexual love, and only medieval Europe accepted that voice as integral to its cultural expression. The twenty or more known Provençal trobairitz, of whom the Countess Beatrice of Die is the most renowned, celebrated as fully and freely as any man the love of the troubadour tradition:

> Handsome friend, charming and kind,
> when shall I have you in my power?
> If only I could lie beside you for an hour
> and embrace you lovingly—
> know this, that I'd give almost anything
> to see you in my husband's place,
> but only under the condition
> that you swear to do my bidding.[14]

Marie de France voiced similar erotic sentiments in her *lais*. Her short tales of romance, often adulterous and always sexual, have caused her to be ranked by Friedrich Heer as one of the "three poets of genius" (along with Chrétien de Troyes and Gautier d'Arras) who created the *roman courtois* of the twelfth century.[15] These two genres, the romance and the lyric, to which women made such significant contributions, make up the corpus of courtly love literature.

In addition to direct literary expression, women promoted the ideas of courtly love by way of patronage and the diversions of their courts. They supported and/or participated in the recitation and singing of poems and romances, and they played out those mock suits, usually presided over by "queens," that settled questions of love. This holds for lesser aristocratic women as well as the great. But great noblewomen, such as Eleanor of Aquitaine and Marie of Champagne, Eleanor's daughter by her first marriage to Louis VII of France, could make their courts major cultural and social centers and play thereby a dominant role in forming the outlook and mores of their class. Eleanor, herself granddaughter of William of Aquitaine, known as the first troubadour, supported the poets and sentiments of Provence at her court in Anjou. When she became Henry II's queen, she brought the literature and manners of courtly love to England. When living apart from Henry at her court in Poitiers, she and her daughter, Marie, taught the arts of courtesy to a number of young women and men who later dispersed to various parts of France, England, Sicily, and Spain, where they constituted the ruling nobility. Some of the most notable authors of the literature of courtly love belonged to these circles. Bernard of Ventadour, one of the outstanding troubadours, sang his poems to none other than the lady Eleanor. Marie de France had connections with the English court of Eleanor and Henry II. Eleanor's daughter, Marie of Champagne, was patron both of Andreas Capellanus, her chaplain, and Chrétien de Troyes, and she may well be responsible for much of the adulterous, frankly sexual behavior the ladies enjoy in the famous works of both. Chrétien claimed he owed to his "lady of Champagne" both "the material and treatment" of Lancelot, which differs considerably in precisely this regard from his earlier and later romances. And Andreas's *De remedio*, the baffling final section of his work that repudiates sexual love and women, may represent not merely a rhetorical tribute to Ovid but a reaction to the pressure of Marie's patronage.[16]

At their courts as in their literature, it would seem that feudal women consciously exerted pressure in shaping the courtly love ideal and making it prevail. But they could do so only because they had actual power to exert. The women who assumed cultural roles as artists and patrons of courtly love had already been assigned political roles that assured them some measure of independence and power. They could and did exercise authority, not merely over the subject laboring population of their lands, but over their own and/or their husbands' vassals. Courtly love, which flourished outside the institution of patriarchal marriage, owed its possibility as well as its model to the dominant political institution of feudal Europe that permitted actual vassal homage to be paid to women.

The Renaissance Lady: Politics and Culture

The kind of economic and political power that supported the cultural activity of feudal noblewomen in the eleventh and twelfth centuries had no counterpart in Renaissance Italy. By the fourteen century, the political units of Italy were mostly sovereign states that regardless of legal claims, recognized no overlords and supported no feudatories. Their nobility held property but no seigniorial power, estates but not jurisdiction. Indeed, in northern and central Italy, a nobility in the European sense hardly existed at all. Down to the coronation of Charles V as Holy Roman Emperor in 1530, there was no Italian king to safeguard the interests of (and thereby limit and control) a "legitimate" nobility that maintained by inheritance traditional prerogatives. Hence, where the urban bourgeoisie did not overthrow the claims of nobility, a despot did, usually in the name of nobility but always for himself. These *signorie*, unlike the bourgeois republics, continued to maintain a landed, military "class" with noble pretensions, but its members increasingly became merely the warriors and ornaments of a court. Hence, the Renaissance aristocrat, who enjoyed neither the independent political powers of feudal jurisdiction nor legally guaranteed status in the ruling estate, either served a despot or became one.

In this sociopolitical context, the exercise of political power by women was far more rare than under feudalism or even under the traditional kind of monarchical state that developed out of feudalism. The two Giovannas of Naples, both queens in their own right, exemplify this latter type of rule. The first, who began her reign in 1343 over Naples and Provence, became in 1356 queen of Sicily as well. Her grandfather, King Robert of Naples—of the same house of Anjou and Provence that hearkens back to Eleanor and to Henry Plantagenet—could and did designate Giovanna as his heir. Similarly, in 1414, Giovanna II became queen of Naples upon the death of her brother. In Naples, in short, women of the ruling house could assume power, not because of their abilities alone, but because the principle of legitimacy continued in force along with the feudal tradition of inheritance by women.

In northern Italy, by contrast, Caterina Sforza ruled her petty principality in typical Renaissance fashion, supported only by the Machiavellian principles of *fortuna* and *virtù* (historical situation and will). Her career, like that of her family, follows the Renaissance pattern of personal and political illegitimacy. Born in

1462, she was an illegitimate daughter of Galeazzo Maria Sforza, heir to the Duchy of Milan. The ducal power of the Sforzas was very recent, dating only from 1450, when Francesco Sforza, illegitimate son of a condottiere and a great condottiere himself, assumed control of the duchy. When his son and heir, Caterina's father, was assassinated after ten years of tyrannous rule, another son, Lodovico, took control of the duchy, first as regent for his nephew (Caterina's half brother), then as outright usurper. Lodovico promoted Caterina's interests for the sake of his own. He married her off at fifteen to a nephew of Pope Sixtus IV, thereby strengthening the alliance between the Sforzas and the Riario family, who now controlled the papacy. The pope carved a state out of papal domains for Caterina's husband, making him Count of Forlì as well as the Lord of Imola, which Caterina brought to the marriage. But the pope died in 1484, her husband died by assassination four years later—and Caterina made the choice to defy the peculiar obstacles posed by Renaissance Italy to a woman's assumption of power.

Once before, with her husband seriously ill at Imola, she had ridden hard to Forlì to quell an incipient coup a day before giving birth. Now at twenty-six, after the assassination of her husband, she and a loyal castellan held the citadel at Forlì against her enemies until Lodovico sent her aid from Milan. Caterina won; she faced down her opponents, who held her six children hostage, then took command as regent for her young son. But her title to rule as regent was inconsequential. Caterina ruled because she mustered superior force and exercised it personally, and to the end she had to exert repeatedly the skill, forcefulness, and ruthless ambition that brought her to power. However, even her martial spirit did not suffice. In the despotisms of Renaissance Italy, where assassinations, coups, and invasions were the order of the day, power stayed closely bound to military force. In 1500, deprived of Milan's support by her uncle Lodovico's deposition, Caterina succumbed to the overwhelming forces of Cesare Borgia and was divested of power after a heroic defense of Forlì.

Because of this political situation, at once statist and unstable, the daughters of the Este, Gonzaga, and Montefeltro families represent women of their class much more than Caterina Sforza did. Their access to power was indirect and provisional, and was expected to be so. In his handbook for the nobility, Baldassare Castiglione's description of the lady of the court makes this difference in sex roles quite clear. On the one hand, the Renaissance lady appears as the equivalent of the courtier. She has the same virtues of mind as he and her education is symmetrical with his. She learns everything—well, almost everything—he does: "knowledge of letters, of music, of painting, and . . . how to dance and how to be festive."[17] Culture is an accomplishment for noblewoman and man alike, used to charm others as much as to develop the self. But for the woman, charm had become the primary occupation and aim. Whereas the courtier's chief task is defined as the profession of arms, "in a Lady who lives at court a certain pleasing affability is becoming above all else, whereby she will be able to entertain graciously every kind of man" (p. 207).

One notable consequence of the Renaissance lady's need to charm is that Castiglione called upon her to give up certain "unbecoming" physical activities such as riding and handling weapons. Granted, he concerned himself with the court lady, as he says, not a queen who may be called upon to rule. But his aestheticizing of the lady's role, his conception of her femaleness as centered in charm, meant that activities such as riding and skill in weaponry would seem unbecoming to women of the ruling families, too. Elisabetta Gonzaga, the idealized duchess of Castiglione's *Courtier*, came close in real life to his normative portrayal of her type. Riding and skill in weaponry had, in fact, no significance for her. The heir to her Duchy of Urbino was decided upon during the lifetime of her husband, and it was this adoptive heir—not the widow of thirty-seven with no children to compete for her care and attention—who assumed power in 1508. Removed from any direct exercise of power, Elisabetta also disregarded the pursuits and pleasures associated with it. Her letters express none of the sense of freedom and daring Caterina Sforza and Beatrice d'Este experienced in riding and the hunt.[18] Altogether, she lacks spirit. Her correspondence shows her to be as docile in adulthood as her early teachers trained her to be. She met adversity, marital and political, with fortitude but never opposed it. She placated father, brother, and husband, and even in Castiglione's depiction of her court, she complied with rather than shaped its conventions.

The differences between Elisabetta Gonzaga and Caterina Sforza are great, yet both personalities were responding to the Renaissance situation of emerging statehood and social mobility. Elisabetta, neither personally illegitimate nor springing from a freebooting condottiere family, was schooled, as Castiglione would have it, away from the martial attitudes and skills requisite for despotic rule. She would not be a prince, she would marry one. Hence, her education, like that of most of the daughters of the ruling families, directed her toward the cultural and social functions of the court. The lady who married a Renaissance prince became a patron. She commissioned works of art and gave gifts for literary works dedicated to her; she drew to her artists and literati. But the court they came to ornament was her husband's, and the culture they represented magnified his princely being, especially when his origins could not. Thus, the Renaissance lady may play an aesthetically significant role in Castiglione's idealized Court of Urbino of 1508, but even he clearly removed her from that equal, to say nothing of superior, position in social discourse that medieval courtly literature had granted her. To the fifteen or so male members of the court whose names he carefully listed, Castiglione admitted only four women to the evening conversations that were the second major occupation at court (the profession of arms, from which he completely excluded women, being the first). Of the four, he distinguished only two women as participants. The Duchess Elisabetta and her companion, Emilia Pia, at least speak, whereas the other two only do a dance. Yet they speak in order to moderate and "direct" discussion by proposing questions and games. They do not themselves contribute to the discussions, and at one point Castiglione relieves them even of their negligible role:

> When signor Gasparo had spoken thus, signora Emilia made a sign to madam Costanza Fregosa, as she sat next in order, that she should speak; and she was making ready to do so, when suddenly the Duchess said: "Since signora Emilia does not choose to go to the trouble of devising a game, it would

be quite right for the other ladies to share in this ease, and thus be exempt from such a burden this evening, especially since there are so many men here that we risk no lack of games." (pp. 19–20)

The men, in short, do all the talking; and the ensuing dialogue on manners and love, as we might expect, is not only developed by men but directed toward their interests.

The contradiction between the professed parity of noble-women and men in *The Courtier* and the merely decorative role Castiglione unwittingly assigned the lady proclaims an important educational and cultural change as well as a political one. Not only did a male ruler preside over the courts of Renaissance Italy, but the court no longer served as arbiter of the cultural functions it did retain. Although restricted to a cultural and social role, she lost dominance in that role as secular education came to require special skills which were claimed as the prerogative of a class of professional teachers. The sons of the Renaissance nobility still pursued their military and diplomatic training in the service of some great lord, but as youths, they transferred their nonmilitary training from the lady to the humanistic tutor or boarding school. In a sense, humanism represented an advance for women as well as for the culture at large. It brought Latin literacy and classical learning to daughters as well as sons of the nobility. But this very development, usually taken as an index of the equality of Renaissance (noble) women with men,[19] spelled a further decline in the lady's influence over courtly society. It placed her as well as her brothers under male cultural authority. The girl of the medieval aristocracy, although unschooled, was brought up at the court of some great lady. Now her brothers' tutors shaped her outlook, male educators who, as humanists, suppressed romance and chivalry to further classical culture, with all its patriarchal and misogynous bias.

The humanistic education of the Renaissance noblewoman helps explain why she cannot compare with her medieval predecessors in shaping a culture responsive to her own interests. In accordance with the new cultural values, the patronage of the Este, Sforza, Gonzaga, and Montefeltro women extended far beyond the literature and art of love and manners, but the works they commissioned, bought, or had dedicated to them do not show any consistent correspondence to their concerns as women. They did not even give noticeable support to women's education, with the single important exception of Battista da Montefeltro, to whom one of the few treatises advocating a humanistic education for women was dedicated. Adopting the universalistic outlook of their humanist teachers, the noblewomen of Renaissance Italy seem to have lost all consciousness of their particular interests as women, while male authors such as Castiglione, who articulated the mores of the Renaissance aristocracy, wrote their works for men. Cultural and political dependency thus combined in Italy to reverse the roles of women and men in developing the new noble code. Medieval courtesy, as set forth in the earliest etiquette books, romances, and rules of love, shaped the man primarily to please the lady. In the thirteenth and fourteenth centuries, rules for women, and strongly patriarchal ones at that, entered French and Italian etiquette books, but not until the Renaissance reformulation of courtly manners and love is it evident how the ways of the lady came to be determined by men in the context of the early modern state. The relation of the sexes here assumed its modern form, and nowhere is this made more visible than in the love relation.

The Renaissance of Chastity

As soon as the literature and values of courtly love made their way into Italy, they were modified in the direction of asexuality. Dante typifies this initial reception of courtly love. His *Vita Nuova*, written in the "sweet new style" (*dolce stil nuovo*) of late-thirteenth-century Tuscany, still celebrates love and the noble heart: "*Amore e 'l cor gentil sono una cosa.*" Love still appears as homage and the lady as someone else's wife. But the lover of Dante's poems is curiously arrested. He frustrates his own desire by rejecting even the aim of union with his beloved. "What is the point of your love for your lady since you are unable to endure her presence?" a lady asks of Dante. "Tell us, for surely the aim of such love must be unique [*novissimo*]!"[20] And novel it is, for Dante confesses that the joy he once took in his beloved's greeting he shall henceforth seek in himself, "in words which praise my lady." Even this understates the case, since Dante's words neither conjure up Beatrice nor seek to melt her. She remains shadowy and remote, for the focus of his poetry has shifted entirely to the subjective pole of love. It is the inner life, *his* inner life, that Dante objectifies. His love poems present a spiritual contest, which he will soon ontologize in the *Divine Comedy*, among competing states of the lover poet's soul.

This dream-world quality expresses in its way a general change that came over the literature of love as its social foundations crumbled. In the north, as the *Romance of the Rose* reminds us, the tradition began to run dry in the late-thirteenth-century period of feudal disintegration—or transformation by the bourgeois economy of the towns and the emergence of the state. And in Provence, after the Albigensian Crusade and the subjection of the Midi to church and crown, Guiraut Riquier significantly called himself the last troubadour. Complaining that "no craft is less esteemed at court than the beautiful mastery of song," he renounced sexual for celestial love and claimed to enter the service of the Virgin Mary.[21] The reception and reworking of the troubadour tradition in Florence of the late 1200s consequently appears somewhat archaic. A conservative, aristocratic nostalgia clings to Dante's love poetry as it does to his political ideas. But if the new social life of the bourgeois commune found little positive representation in his poetry, Florence did drain from his poems the social content of feudal experience. The lover as knight or trobairitz thus gave way to a poet scholar. The experience of a wandering, questing life gave way to scholastic interests, to distinguishing and classifying states of feeling. And the courtly celebration of romance, modeled upon vassalage and enjoyed in secret meetings, became a private circulation of poems analyzing the spiritual effects of unrequited love.

The actual disappearance of the social world of the court and its presiding lady underlies the disappearance of sex and the physical evaporation of the woman in these poems. The ladies of the romances and troubadour poetry may be stereotypically blond, candid, and fair, but their authors meant them to be taken as physically and socially "real." In the love poetry of Dante, and of Petrarch and Vittoria Colonna, who continue his tradition, the beloved may just as well be dead—and, indeed, all three authors made them so. They have no meaningful, objective existence, and not merely because their affective experience lacks a voice. This would hold for troubadour poetry too, since the lyric, unlike the romance, articulates only the feelings of the lover. The unreality of the Renaissance beloved has rather to do with the *quality* of the Renaissance lover's feelings. As former social relations that sustained mutuality and interaction among lovers vanished, the lover fell back on a narcissistic experience. The Dantesque beloved merely inspires feelings that have no outer, physical aim; or, they have a transcendent aim that the beloved merely mediates. In either case, love casts off sexuality. Indeed, the role of the beloved as mediator is asexual in a double sense, as the *Divine Comedy* shows. Not only does the beloved never respond sexually to the lover, but the feelings she arouses in him turn into a spiritual love that makes of their entire relationship a mere symbol or allegory.

Interest even in this shadowy kind of romance dropped off markedly as the work of Dante, Petrarch, and Boccaccio led into the fifteenth-century renaissance of Graeco-Roman art and letters. The Florentine humanists in particular appropriated only the classical side of their predecessors' thought, the side that served public concerns. They rejected the dominance of love in human life, along with the inwardness and seclusion of the religious, the scholar, and the lovesick poet. Dante, for example, figured primarily as a citizen to his biographer, Lionardo Bruni, who, as humanist chancellor of Florence, made him out as a modern Socrates, at once a political figure, a family man, and a rhetor: an exemplar for the new polis.[22] Only in relation to the institution of the family did Florentine civic humanism take up questions of love and sexuality. In this context, they developed the bourgeois sex-role system, placing man in the public sphere and the patrician woman in the home, requiring social virtues from him and chastity and motherhood from her. In bourgeois Florence, the humanists would have nothing to do with the old aristocratic tradition of relative social and sexual parity. In the petty Italian despotisms, however, and even in Florence under the princely Lorenzo de' Medici late in the fifteenth century, the traditions and culture of the nobility remained meaningful.[23] Castiglione's *Courtier*, and the corpus of Renaissance works it heads, took up the themes of love and courtesy for this courtly society, adapting them to contemporary social and cultural needs. Yet in this milieu, too, within the very tradition of courtly literature, new constraints upon female sexuality emerged. Castiglione, the single most important spokesman of Renaissance love and manners, retained in his love theory Dante's two basic features: the detachment of love from sexuality and the allegorization of the love theme. Moreover, he introduced into the aristocratic conception of sex roles some of the patriarchal notions of women's confinement to the family that bourgeois humanists had been restoring.

Overtly, as we saw, Castiglione and his class supported a complementary conception of sex roles, in part because a nobility that did no work at all gave little thought to a sexual division of labor. He could thus take up the late medieval *querelle des femmes* set off by the *Romance of the Rose* and debate the question of women's dignity much to their favor. Castiglione places Aristotle's (and Aquinas's) notion of woman as a defective man in the mouth of an aggrieved misogynist, Gasparo; he criticizes Plato's low regard for women, even though he did permit them to govern in *The Republic*; he rejects Ovid's theory of love as not "gentle" enough. Most significantly, he opposes Gasparo's bourgeois notion of women's exclusively domestic role. Yet for all this, Castiglione established in *The Courtier* a fateful bond between love and marriage. One index of a heightened patriarchal outlook among the Renaissance nobility is that love in the usual emotional and sexual sense must lead to marriage and be confined to it—for women, that is.

The issue gets couched, like all others in the book, in the form of a debate. There are pros and cons; but the prevailing view is unmistakable. If the ideal court lady loves, she should love someone whom she can marry. If married, and the mishap befalls her "that her husband's hate or another's love should bring her to love, I would have her give her lover a spiritual love only; nor must she ever give him any sure sign of her love, either by word or gesture or by other means that can make him certain of it" (p. 263). *The Courtier* thus takes a strange, transitional position on the relations among love, sex, and marriage, which bourgeois Europe would later fuse into one familial whole. Responding to a situation of general female dependency among the nobility, and to the restoration of patriarchal family values, at once classical and bourgeois, Castiglione, like Renaissance love theorists in general, connected love and marriage. But facing the same realities of political marriage and clerical celibacy that beset the medieval aristocracy, he still focused upon the love that takes place outside it. On this point, too, however, he broke with the courtly love tradition. He proposed on the one hand a Neo-Platonic notion of spiritual love, and on the other, the double standard.[24]

Castiglione's image of the lover is interesting in this regard. Did he think his suppression of female sexual love would be more justifiable if he had a churchman, Pietro Bembo (elevated to cardinal in 1539), enunciate the new theory and had him discourse upon the love of an aging courtier rather than that of a young knight? In any case, adopting the Platonic definition of love as desire to enjoy beauty, Bembo located this lover in a metaphysical and physical hierarchy between sense ("below") and intellect ("above"). As reason mediates between the physical and the spiritual, so man, aroused by the visible beauty of his beloved, may direct his desire beyond her to the true, intelligible source of her beauty. He may, however, also turn toward sense. Young men fall into this error, and we should expect it of them, Bembo explains in the Neo-Platonic language of the Florentine philosopher Marsilio Ficino. "For finding itself deep in an earthly prison, and deprived of spiritual contemplation in exercising its office of governing the body, the soul of itself cannot clearly perceive the truth; wherefore, in order to have knowledge, it is obliged to turn to the senses . . . and so it believes them . . . and lets itself be guided by them, especially when they have so much vigor that they almost force it" (pp. 338–339). A misdirection of the soul leads to sexual union (though obviously not with the court lady). The preferred kind of union, achieved by way of ascent, uses love of the lady as a step toward love of universal beauty. The lover here ascends from awareness of his own human spirit, which responds to beauty, to awareness of that universal intellect that comprehends universal beauty. Then, "transformed into an angel," his soul finds supreme happiness in divine love. Love may hereby soar to an ontologically noble end, and the beauty of the woman who inspires such ascent may acquire metaphysical status and dignity. But Love, Beauty, Woman, aestheticized as Botticelli's Venus and given cosmic import, were in effect denatured, robbed of body, sex, and passion by this elevation. The simple kiss of love-service became a rarefied kiss of the soul: "A man delights in joining his mouth to that of his beloved in a kiss, not in order to bring himself to any unseemly desire, but because he feels that that bond is the opening of mutual access to their souls" (pp. 349–350). And instead of initiating love, the kiss now terminated physical contact, at least for the churchman and/or aging courtier who sought an ennobling experience—and for the woman obliged to play her role as lady.

Responsive as he still was to medieval views of love, Castiglione at least debated the issue of the double standard. His spokesmen point out that men make the rules permitting themselves and not women sexual freedom, and that concern for legitimacy does not justify this inequality. Since these same men claim to be more virtuous than women, they could more easily restrain themselves. In that case, "there would be neither more nor less certainty about offspring, for even if women were unchaste, they could in no way bear children of themselves . . . provided men were continent and did not take part in the unchastity of women" (pp. 240–241). But for all this, the book supplies an excess of hortatory tales about female chastity, and in the section of the dialogue granting young men indulgence in sensual love, no one speaks for young women, who ought to be doubly "prone," as youths and as women, according to the views of the time.

This is theory, of course. But one thinks of the examples: Eleanor of Aquitaine changing bedmates in the midst of a crusade; Elisabetta Gonzaga, so constrained by the conventions of her own court that she would not take a lover even though her husband was impotent. She, needless to say, figures as Castiglione's prime exemplar: "Our Duchess who has lived with her husband for fifteen years like a widow" (p. 253). Bembo, on the other hand, in the years before he became cardinal, lived with and had three children by Donna Morosina. But however they actually lived, in the new ideology a spiritualized noble love *supplemented* the experience of men while it *defined* extramarital experience for the lady. For women, chastity had become the convention of the Renaissance courts, signaling the twofold fact that the dominant institutions of sixteenth-century Italian society would not support the adulterous sexuality of courtly love, and that women, suffering a relative loss of power within these institutions, could not at first make them responsive to their needs. Legitimacy is a significant factor here. Even courtly love had paid some deference to it (and to the desire of women to avoid conception) by restraining intercourse while promoting romantic and sexual play. But now, with cultural and political power held almost entirely by men, the norm of female chastity came to express the concerns of Renaissance noblemen as they moved into a new situation as a hereditary, dependent class.

This changed situation of the aristocracy accounts both for Castiglione's widespread appeal and for his telling transformation of the love relation. Because *The Courtier* created a mannered way of life that could give to a dependent nobility a sense of self-sufficiency, of inner power and control, which they had lost in a real economic and political sense, the book's popularity spread from Italy through Europe at large in the sixteenth and seventeenth centuries. Although set in the Urbino court of 1508, it was actually begun some ten years after that and published in 1528—after the sack of Rome, and at a time when the princely states of Italy and Europe were coming to resemble each other more closely than they had in the fourteenth and fifteenth centuries. The monarchs of Europe, consolidating and centralizing their states, were at once protecting the privileges of their nobility and suppressing feudal power.[25] Likewise in Italy, as the entire country fell under the hegemony of Charles V, the nobility began to be stabilized. Throughout sixteenth-century Italy, new laws began to limit and regulate membership in a hereditary aristocratic class, prompting a new concern with legitimacy and purity of the blood. Castiglione's demand for female chastity in part responds to this particular concern. His theory of love as a whole responds to the general situation of the Renaissance nobility. In the discourse on love for which he made Bembo the spokesman, he brought to the love relation the same psychic attitudes with which he confronted the political situation. Indeed, he used the love relation as a symbol to convey his sense of political relations.

The changed times to which Castiglione refers in his introduction he experienced as a condition of servitude. The dominant problem of the sixteenth-century Italian nobility, like that of the English nobility under the Tudors, had become one of obedience. As one of Castiglione's courtiers expressed it, God had better grant them "good masters, for, once we have them, we have to endure them as they are" (p. 116). It is this transformation of aristocratic service to statism, which gave rise to Castiglione's leading idea of nobility as courtiers, that shaped his theory of love as well. Bembo's aging courtier, passionless in his rational love, sums up the theme of the entire book: how to maintain by detachment the sense of self now threatened by the loss of independent power. The soul in its earthly prison, the courtier in his social one, renounce the power of self-determination that has in fact been denied them. They renounce *wanting* such power; "If the flame is extinguished, the danger is also extinguished" (p. 347). In love, as in service, the courtier preserves independence by avoiding desire for real love, real power. He does not touch or allow himself to be touched by either. "To enjoy beauty without suffering, the Courtier, aided by reason, must turn his desire entirely away from the body and to beauty alone, [to] contemplate it in its simple and pure self" (p. 351). He may gaze at the object of his love-service, he may listen, but there he reaches the limits of the actual physical relation and transforms her beauty, or the prince's power, into a pure idea. "Spared the bitterness and calamities" of thwarted passion thereby, he loves and serves an image only. The courtier gives obeisance, but only to a reality of his own making: "for he will always carry his precious treasure with him, shut up in his heart, and will also, by the force of his own imagination, make her beauty [or the prince's power] much more beautiful than in reality it is" (p. 352).

Thus, the courtier can serve and not serve, love and not love. He can even attain the relief of surrender by making use of this inner love-service "as a step" to mount to a more sublime sense of service. Contemplation of the Idea the courtier has discovered within his own soul excites a purified desire to love, to serve, to unite with intellectual beauty (or power). Just as love guided his soul from the particular beauty of his beloved to the universal concept, love of that intelligible beauty (or power) glimpsed within transports the soul from the self, the particular intellect, to the universal intellect. Aflame with an utterly spiritual love (or a spiritualized sense of service), the soul then "understands all things intelligible, and without any veil or cloud views the wide sea of pure divine beauty, and receives it into itself, enjoying that supreme happiness of which the senses are incapable" (p. 354). What does this semimystical discourse teach but that by "true" service, the courtier may break out of his citadel of independence, his inner aloofness, to rise and surrender to the pure idea of Power? What does his service become but a freely chosen Obedience, which he can construe as the supreme virtue? In both its sublimated acceptance or resignation and its inner detachment from the actual, Bembo's discourse on love exemplifies the relation between subject and state, obedience and power, that runs through the entire book. Indeed, Castiglione regarded the monarch's power exactly as he had Bembo present the lady's beauty, as symbolic of God: "As in the heavens the sun and the moon and the other stars exhibit to the world a certain likeness of God, so on earth a much liker image of God is seen in . . . princes." Clearly, if "men have been put by God under princes" (p. 307), if they have been placed under princes as under His image, what end can be higher than service in virtue, than the purified experience of Service?

The likeness of the lady to the prince in this theory, her elevation to the pedestal of Neo-Platonic love, both masks and expresses the new dependency of the Renaissance noblewoman. In a structured hierarchy of superior and inferior, she seems to be served by the courtier. But this love theory really made her serve—and stand as a symbol of how the relation of domination may be reversed, so that the prince could be made to serve the interests of the courtier. The Renaissance lady is not desired, not loved for herself. Rendered passive and chaste, she merely mediates the courtier's safe transcendence of an otherwise demeaning necessity. On the plane of symbolism, Castiglione thus had the courtier dominate both her and the prince; and on the plane of reality, he indirectly acknowledged the courtier's actual domination of the lady by having him adopt "woman's ways" in his relations to the prince. Castiglione had to defend against effeminacy in the courtier, both the charge of it (p. 92) and the actuality of faces "soft and feminine as many attempt to have who not only curl their hair and pluck their eyebrows, but preen themselves . . . and appear so tender and languid . . . and utter their words so limply" (p. 36). Yet the close-fitting costume of the Renaissance nobleman displayed the courtier exactly as Castiglione would have him, "well built and shapely of limb" (p. 36). His clothes set off his grace, as did his nonchalant ease, the new manner of those "who seem in words, laughter, in posture not to care" (p. 44). To be attractive, accomplished, and seem not to care; to charm and do so coolly—how concerned with impression, how masked the true self. And how manipulative: petitioning his lord, the courtier knows to be "discreet in choosing the occasion, and will ask things that are proper and reasonable; and he will so frame his request, omitting those parts that he knows can cause displeasure, and will skillfully make easy the difficult points so that his lord will always grant it" (p. 111). In short, how like a woman—or a dependent, for that is the root of the simile.

The accommodation of the sixteenth- and seventeenth century courtier to the ways and dress of women in no way bespeaks a greater parity between them. It reflects, rather, that general restructuring of social relations that entailed for the Renaissance noblewoman a greater dependency upon men as feudal independence and reciprocity yielded to the state. In this new situation, the entire nobility suffered a loss. Hence, the courtier's posture of dependency, his concern with the pleasing impression, his resolve "to perceive what his prince likes, and . . . to bend himself to this" (pp. 110–111). But as the state overrode aristocratic power, the lady suffered a double loss. Deprived of the possibility of independent power that the combined interests of kinship and feudalism guaranteed some women in the Middle Ages, and that the states of early modern Europe would preserve in part, the Italian noblewoman in particular entered a relation of almost universal dependence upon her family and her husband. And she experienced this dependency at the same time as she lost her commanding position with respect to the secular culture of her society.

Hence, the love theory of the Italian courts developed in ways as indifferent to the interests of women as the courtier, in his self-sufficiency, was indifferent as a lover. It accepted, as medieval courtly love did not, the double standard. It bound the lady to chastity, to the merely procreative sex of political marriage, just as her weighty and costly costume came to conceal and constrain her body while it displayed her husband's noble rank. Indeed, the person of the woman became so inconsequential to this love relation that one doubted whether she could love at all. The question that emerges at the end of *The Courtier* as to "whether or not women are as capable of divine love as men" (p. 350) belongs to a love theory structured by mediation rather than mutuality. Woman's beauty inspired love but the lover, the agent, was man. And the question stands unresolved at the end of *The Courtier*—because at heart the spokesmen for Renaissance love were not really concerned about women or love at all.

Where courtly love had used the social relation of vassalage to work out a genuine concern with sexual love, Castiglione's thought moved in exactly the opposite direction. He allegorized love as fully as Dante did, using the relation of the sexes to symbolize the new political order. In this, his love theory reflects the social realities of the Renaissance. The denial of the right and power of women to love, the transformation of women into passive "others" who serve, fits the self-image of the courtier, the one Castiglione sought to remedy. The symbolic relation of the sexes thus mirrors the new social relations of the state, much as courtly love displayed the feudal relations of reciprocal personal dependence. But Renaissance love reflects, as well, the actual condition of dependency suffered by noblewomen as the state arose. If the courtier who charms the prince bears the same relation to him as the lady bears to the courtier, it is because Castiglione understood the relation of the sexes in the same terms that he used to describe the political relation: i.e., as a relation between servant and lord. The nobleman suffered this relation in the public domain only. The lady, denied access to a freely chosen, mutually satisfying love relation, suffered it in the personal domain as well. Moreover, Castiglione's theory, unlike the courtly love it superseded, subordinated love itself to the public concerns of the Renaissance nobleman. He set forth the relation of the sexes as one of dependency and domination, but he did so in order to express and deal with the political relation and its problems. The personal values of love, which the entire feudality once prized, were henceforth increasingly left to the lady. The courtier formed his primary bond with the modern prince.

In sum, a new division between personal and public life made itself felt as the state came to organize Renaissance society, and with that division the modern relation of the sexes made its appearance,[26] even among the Renaissance nobility. Noblewomen, too, were increasingly removed from public concerns—economic, political, and cultural—and although they did not disappear into a private realm of family and domestic concerns as fully as their sisters in the patrician bourgeoisie, their loss of public power made itself felt in new constraints placed upon their personal as well as their social lives. Renaissance ideas on love and manners, more classical than medieval, and almost exclusively a male product, expressed this new subordination of women to the interests of husbands and male-dominated kin groups and served to justify the removal of women from an "unladylike" position of power and erotic independence. All the advances of Renaissance Italy, its protocapitalist economy, its states, and its humanistic culture, worked to mold the noblewoman into an aesthetic object: decorous, chaste, and doubly dependent—on her husband as well as the prince.

Notes

1. The traditional view of the equality of Renaissance women with men goes back to Jacob Burckhardt's classic, *The Civilization of the Renaissance in Italy* (1860). It has found its way into most general histories of women, such as Mary Beard's *Women as Force in History* (1946), Simone de Beauvoir's *The Second Sex* (1949), and Emily James Putnam's *The Lady* (1910), although the latter is a sensitive and sophisticated treatment. It also dominates most histories of Renaissance women, the best of which is E. Rodocanachi, *La femme italienne avant, pendant et après la Renaissance*, Hachette, Paris, 1922. A notable exception is Ruth Kelso, *Doctrine for the Lady of the Renaissance*, University of Illinois Press, Urbana, 1956, who discovered there was no such parity.

2. The major Renaissance statement of the bourgeois domestication of women was made by Leon Battista Alberti in Book 3 of *Della Famiglia* (c. 1435), which is a free adaptation of the Athenian situation described by Xenophon in the *Oeconomicus*.

3. Andreas Capellanus, *The Art of Courtly Love*, trans. John J. Parry, Columbia University Press, New York, 1941, pp. 150–151.

4. Maurice Valency, *In Praise of Love: An Introduction to the Love-Poetry of the Renaissance*, Macmillan, New York, 1961, p. 146.

5. *"E il dompna deu a son drut far honor/Cum ad amic, mas non cum a seignor."* Ibid., p. 64.

6. Lanval (Sir Launfal), *Les lais de Marie de France*, ed. Paul Tuffrau, L'Edition d'Art H. Piazza, Paris, n.d., p. 41. English ed., *Lays of Marie de France*, J. M. Dent and E. P. Dutton, London and New York, 1911.

7. Excellent trans. and ed. by W. W. Comfort, *Arthurian Romances*, Dent and Dutton Everyman's Library, London and New York, 1970, p. 286.

8. Thomas Aquinas, *Summa Theologiae*, pt. 1–2, q. 28, art. 5.

9. Lanval, *Les lais*, p. 10.

10. Thomas Frederick Crane, *Italian Social Customs of the Sixteenth Century*, Yale University Press, New Haven, 1920, pp. 10–11.

11. As Marc Bloch pointed out, the great French principalities that no longer required personal military service on the part of their holders were among the first to be passed on to women when male heirs were wanting. *Feudal Society*, trans. L. A. Manyon, University of Chicago Press, Chicago, 1964, p. 201.

12. David Herlihy, "Land, Family and Women in Continental Europe, 701–1200," *Traditio*, 18 (1962), 89–120. Also, "Women in Medieval Society," *The Smith History Lecture*, University of St. Thomas, Texas, 1971. For a fine new work on abbesses, see Joan Morris, *The Lady Was a Bishop*, Collier and Macmillan, New York and London, 1973. Marie de France may have been an abbess of Shaftesbury.

13. Emily James Putnam, *The Lady*, University of Chicago Press, Chicago and London, 1970, p. 118. See also the chapter on the abbess in the same book.

14. From *The Women Troubadours*, trans. and ed. by Meg Bogin, Paddington Press, New York/London, 1976.

15. Friedrich Heer, *The Medieval World: Europe 1100–1350*, Mentor Books, New York, 1963, pp. 167, 178–179.

16. This was Amy Kelly's surmise in "Eleanor of Aquitaine and Her Courts of Love," *Speculum*, 12 (January 1937), 3–19.

17. From *The Book of the Courtier*, by Baldesar Castiglione, a new translation by Charles S. Singleton (New York: Doubleday, 1959), p. 20. Copyright © 1959 by Charles S. Singleton and Edgar de N. Mayhew. This and other quotations throughout the chapter are reprinted by permission of Doubleday & Co., Inc.

18. Selections from the correspondence of Renaissance noblewomen can be found in the biographies listed in the bibliography.

19. An interesting exception is W. Ong's "Latin Language Study as a Renaissance Puberty Rite," *Studies in Philology*, 56 (1959), 103–124; also Margaret Leah King's "The Religious Retreat of Isotta Nogarola (1418–1466)," *Signs*, Summer 1978.

20. Dante Alighieri, *La Vita Nuova*, trans. Barbara Reynolds, Penguin Books, Middlesex, England and Baltimore, 1971, poem 18.

21. Frederick Goldin, trans., *Lyrics of the Troubadours and Trouvères*, Doubleday, New York, 1973, p. 325.

22. David Thompson and Alan F. Nagel, eds. and trans., *The Three Crowns of Florence: Humanist Assessments of Dante, Petrarca, and Boccaccio*, Harper & Row, New York, 1972.

23. For Renaissance humanistic and courtly literature, Vittorio Rossi, *Il quattrocento*, F. Vallardi, Milan, 1933; Ruth Kelso, *Doctrine for the Lady of the Renaissance*, University of Illinois Press, Urbana, 1956. On erotic life, interesting remarks by David Herlihy, "Some Psychological and Social Roots of Violence in the Tuscan Cities," *Violence and Civil Disorder in Italian Cities, 1200–1500*, ed. Lauro Martines, University of California Press, Berkeley, 1972, pp. 129–154.

24. For historical context, Keith Thomas, "The Double Standard," *Journal of the History of Ideas*, 20 (1959), 195–216; N. J. Perella, *The Kiss Sacred and Profane: An Interpretive History of Kiss Symbolism*, University of California Press, Berkeley, 1969; Morton Hunt, *The Natural History of Love*, Funk & Wagnalls, New York, 1967.

25. Fernand Braudel, *The Mediterranean World*, Routledge & Kegan Paul, London, 1973; A. Ventura, *Nobiltà e popolo nella società Veneta*, Laterza, Bari, 1964; Lawrence Stone, *The Crisis of the Aristocracy, 1558–1641*, Clarendon Press, Oxford, 1965.

26. The status of women as related to the distinction of public and private spheres of activity in various societies is a key idea in most of the anthropological studies in *Women, Culture, and Society*, eds. Michelle Zimbalist Rosaldo and Louise Lamphere, Stanford University Press, Stanford, 1974.

Suggestions for Further Reading

On Renaissance women: Stanley Chojnacki, "Patrician Women in Early Renaissance Venice," *Studies in the Renaissance*, 21 (1974), 1976–203; Susan Groag Bell, "Christine de Pizan," *Feminist Studies*, 3 (Spring/Summer 1976), 173–184; Joan Kelly-Gadol, "Notes on Women in the Renaissance," *Conceptual Frameworks in Women's History* (Sarah Lawrence Publications, Bronxville, N.Y., 1976); Margaret Leah King, "The Religious Retreat of Isotta Nogarola," *Signs*, Summer 1978; Kathleen Casey, "Reconstructing the Experience of Medieval Woman," *Liberating Women's History*, ed. Berenice Carroll (University of Illinois Press, Urbana, 1976), 224–249. With the exception of Ruth Kelso, *Doctrine for the Lady of the Renaissance* (University of Illinois Press, Urbana, 1956), and Ernst Breisach, *Caterina Sforza: A Renaissance Virago* (University of Chicago Press, Chicago, 1967), all other serious studies stem from the first wave of the feminist movement. They form a necessary basis, although they concern themselves almost exclusively with "exceptional" women and are not sensitive to socioeconomic factors. Among them, Marian Andrews (pseud. Christopher Hare), *The Most Illustrious Ladies of the Italian Renaissance* (Scribner's, New York, 1904); Julia Cartwright (Mrs. Ady), *Isabella d'Este*, 2 vols. (Dutton, New York, 1903) and *Beatrice d'Este* (1899); Ferdinand Gregorovius, *Lucrezia Borgia* (Blom, 1968 reprint of 1903 ed.); E. Rodocanachi, *La femme italienne avant, pendant et après la Renaissance* (Hachette, Paris, 1922); T. A. Trollope, *A Decade of Italian Women*, 2 vols. (Chapman & Hall, London, 1859).

The most significant studies in demographic and social history bearing upon Renaissance women are those of David Herlihy, among whose several articles are "Mapping Households in Medieval Italy," *The Catholic Historical Review*, 58 (April 1972), 1–24; "Viellir à Florence au Quattrocento," *Annales*, 24 (November–December 1969), 1338–1352; "The Tuscan Town in the Quattrocento," *Medievalia et Humanistica*, 1 (1970),

81–110; also, a forthcoming book on the Tuscan family. Two demographic studies on infanticide and foundlings in Florence by Richard C. Trexler are in *History of Childhood Quarterly*, 1, nos. 1 and 2 (1973); Gene Brucker has excellent selections from wills, marriage contracts, government minutes, legal judgments, etc., in *The Society of Renaissance Florence: A Documentary Study* (Harper, New York, 1971).

Histories of family life and childrearing among the courtly aristocracy of early modern France supplement very nicely Castiglione's portrayal of the courtier and court lady. Among them, Philippe Ariès, *Centuries of Childhood: A Social History of Family Life* (Knopf, New York, 1965), and David Hunt, *Parents and Children in History* (Harper, New York, 1972). Although he does not deal with Renaissance Italy, Lawrence Stone's *The Crisis of the Aristocracy, 1558–1641* (Clarendon Press, Oxford, 1965) is indispensable reading for information about aristocratic social life.

Primary sources on medieval and Renaissance love used in the text in English translation are: Andreas Capellanus, *The Art of Courtly Love* (trans. John J. Parry, Columbia University Press, New York, 1941); *Lays of Marie de France* (J. M. Dent and E. P. Dutton, London and New York, 1911); Chrétien de Troyes's Lancelot from *Arthurian Romances* (trans. and ed. W. W. Comfort, Dent and Dutton Everyman's Library, London and New York, 1970); Baldassare Castiglione, *The Book of the Courtier* (trans. Charles S. Singleton, Doubleday, New York, 1959); Dante Alighieri, *La Vita Nuova* (trans. Barbara Reynolds, Penguin Books, Middlesex, England and Baltimore, 1971). See, too, F. X. Newman, *The Meaning of Courtly Love* (The State University of New York Press, Albany, 1967), for contemporary opinion and a good bibliography. The soundest and most sensitive study is still Maurice Valency's *In Praise of Love* (Macmillan, New York, 1961). Two fine articles on the literature of love, sex, and marriage in early modern Europe are by William Haller, "Hail Wedded Love," *A Journal of English Literary History*, 13 (June 1946), 79–97, and Paul Siegel, "The Petrarchan Sonneteers and Neo-Platonic Love," *Studies in Philology*, 42 (1945), 164–182.

THREE

The Doubled Vision of Feminist Theory

A Postscript to the "Women and Power" Conference

*F*eminist theory is today bringing about a major advance in social vision. If we take as an index of the reemergence of feminist theory Juliet Mitchell's 1966 essay on the four structures by which to assess "woman's estate,"[1] we can appreciate how our understanding of women and society has developed. For more than a decade, the women's movement has been confronting sex oppression in the domains she helped name for us—production, reproduction, sexuality, and socialization. Since 1966 we have struggled personally, intellectually, and politically against the socializing of girls/women into the servicing, mother role, and against the socializing of boys/men into requiring it. We have moved in thought, feeling, and action against the restriction of female sexuality to phallus and family. We have struggled to understand how and why male-dominant institutions control biological and social reproduction, and we have been fighting that control. And we have moved in several ways against an organization of work that fosters and profits from the sexual division of labor and the unequal relation of the sexes that flows from it. In practice and consciousness, this phase of the women's movement is no longer where it was when Juliet Mitchell marked out the paths along which we did in-

Reprinted from *Feminist Studies* 5, no. 1 (Spring 1979): 216–27.
© 1979 Feminist Studies, Inc.

deed move: and our theoretical understanding has developed accordingly.

Responding to women's changed, and rapidly changing social situation and consciousness, feminist theory is now at a point where a significant transformation in social vision is both called for and being accomplished. What I propose to do here is characterize an aspect of this advance in theoretical outlook that I see emerging out of the several schools and strands of feminist thought and scholarship. It consists of what I call a unified "doubled" view of the social order, and it promises to overcome certain conflicts in theory and practice that stem from earlier notions of sex oppression and social change.

Two Sociosexual Spheres

In examining the sex order (or sex/gender system) of our society, recent feminist theory has shown how the industrial world of the nineteenth and early twentieth centuries construed society as divided into two sociosexual spheres. The bourgeois conception of a private and a public domain, a domain of work and one of leisure, also separated the sexes. Settling women and men into their respective spheres of home and work, it defined the place and roles of the sexes as separate and "complementary."

Our understanding of this view, and its implications for women, has been clarified by virtually all feminist scholarship. Feminist thinkers in the Marxist tradition[2] have traced the divided sociosexual order to the organization of capitalist production outside the home. They have shown how the separation of work (production) from leisure (consumption) really exists for men only. As a conception of society, the notion of home as a refuge from the world of work masks a sexual division of labor. It mystifies women's work in the home, obscuring the fact that this domestic labor helps "reproduce" capitalist and patriarchal society. I.e., procreation and the daily work that goes into consumption (housework) and socialization (childrearing) in the private family sustains the working population: trains people to know and keep their place: and provides for their replacement. At the same time, this unwaged and unacknowledged work of women in the home keeps women dependent on men and bound to a subordinate, servicing role.

Radical feminists,[3] concerned more with sexuality and social-ization than with labor, have supplemented this analysis. Focus-ing upon consciousness and culture on the one hand, as well as the obscure levels of the unconscious, they have analyzed the psychic, sexual, and ideological structures that differentiate the sexes, setting up an antagonistic relation of dominance and sub-jection between them. We owe to this tradition our understand-ing of gender, of the lived inequalities of the "complementary" sex order, and how those inequalities are perpetuated by casting all women into the role of Mother.

With different emphases, one on societal structures, the other on psychic-sexual ones, both the radical and socialist currents of feminist thought thus point to the centrality of *reproduction* in women's lives. The defining of women as reproductive beings— as housewives and mothers—is seen as shaping women's self-image and sense of worth; sexual preference and expression; and women's relations with other women, with children, and men. In the Marxist inspired analysis, women's work of biolog-ical and social reproduction in the home (procreation and do-mestic labor) is seen as supporting an economic, social, and political order dominated by men, while at the same time pre-venting women from participating directly in that order. Indus-trial society made women marginal to the realm of production as it developed. It excluded women from the modern state. And "official" thought and culture, shaped by the male-dominant in-stitutions of Church and Academy, sought to legitimate this so-ciosexual division by justifying the confinement of women to their separate sphere.[4]

To define the present state of feminist theory, it is important to note that in the nineteenth and early twentieth centuries, even opponents of the prevailing social order accepted in certain ways its establishment of two sexual social domains. This lim-ited feminist and socialist theories of sex oppression, putting them in conflict with each other at certain points, and in internal conflict as well. To be sure, the different experience of middle-class and working women is reflected in the emphasis one theory put on gender and the other placed on class. But that feminists in the liberal/radical line of thought (as set forth by Harriet Taylor, for example) should generally ascribe the subjection of women to the "personal" satisfactions of male privilege,[5] while

socialists saw it rooted in the property arrangements of class society, also points to conceptual difficulties in arriving at a view
that would encompass the situation of all women.

This difficulty is especially evident in nineteenth-century socialist theory, which sought to be genuinely comprehensive on
the Woman Question. It attempted an analysis of sex and class,
and of the public and private domains. But it was never able to
"see" sex/class operating simultaneously in both realms. Marxist
thought on women, as developed by Engels and Bebel, found in
the propertyless condition of the modern wage-earning family
the material basis (and not just a basis) for the liberation of
women. Once the productive property that was now held privately by the families of the bourgeoisie was publicly owned,
there would be no patrimony to bind middle-class women to reproduction of the patrilineage. Nor would there be poverty that
was forcing working women into sexual service to men. Although this view covered the different situation of both groups
of women, it was not adequate to explain either the nature of sex
oppression or its causes. Sex oppression was taken to be "private," as having to do only with sexuality and procreation, while
causes were all in the "public" domain of capitalism's productive
relations. Many socialist feminists developed more complex
views. Crystal Eastman, for example, was sharply aware of sex
hierarchy in the work force and of male domination in the socialist movement.[6] But the mainstream of Marxist views on the
"Woman Question" did not become responsive to the issue of
sex hierarchy in social production and social organization, and
it continued to regard male interest in the subordination of
women (independent of property) as vestigial only.[7]

In addition to differences between socialists and feminists,
and between the claims of sex and class, other currents of feminist thought expressed other versions of the divided sociosexual
world. Many feminists came in different ways to defend and
prize the so-called female realm and its values. In the voluntary
motherhood circles, e.g., and even among suffragists and free
lovers, as Linda Gordon has shown, traditional sex roles were
generally accepted.[8] While resisting male control over sexuality
and reproduction, over what they themselves took to be their
"natural" domain, many of these women sought to deepen ap-

preciation of family, motherhood, and/or the particular virtues of Woman. Even some socialist women held similar notions, maintaining that socialism would simply make it possible for all women to lead domestic, mothering lives.[9]

In somewhat different form, these conflicting tendencies still divide the contemporary women's movement and feminist theory. In the United States, we oscillate between participating in, and separating from, organizations and institutions that remain alienating and stubbornly male dominant. We are pulled in one direction by a Marxist-feminist analysis of the socioeconomic bases of women's oppression, and in another direction by a radical feminist focus on male control of women's bodies as the key to patriarchy. Our differences have not hampered the ad hoc coalitions formed around struggles for abortion and protection against sterilization abuse; for affirmative action, maternity leave, and daycare; for the Equal Rights Amendment and the right of sexual preference. But differences in theoretical position do affect our broader social commitments and political alliances. They affect our conception of the scope of the women's movement; its relation to issues of race and class; and specifically, whether or how to join with what are still male-dominant movements of resistance to inequities stemming from an imperialist organization of the world economy and society.

Women will not forget how this phase of the women's movement was forced to repeat the first wave in its inception. Women's groups developed out of the radical movements of the 1960s much as they did in the 1840s and 50s when women from the abolition and peace movements came to form their own organizations because men, in those very movements against oppression, retained sex-oppressive structures and behavior. It is when we remember this that we feel the strongest temptation to stay within the supportive network of our women's groups, to restructure our relationships along nonhierarchical lines, to live our own women's culture. The tension between the need for separation and the will to create social change runs deep in the women's movement and in each of our lives, as do the related tensions between the claims of class, race, and sex.[10] It is my belief that we will live with these tensions for a long time. We will live with them perhaps as long as there is race, class, and sex oppression. For the truth is that the women's movement encompasses all these positions. We need both separation and full social participation to liberate ourselves from our several forms of sex oppression; and sex oppression will not itself be overcome without liberation from all forms of domination and hierarchy.

To say this does not resolve these oppositions. But it may urge us toward other ways of conceiving them. It helps us feel in practical terms the course that feminist theory needs to take and, I believe, is taking. Indeed, the argument I want to make here is that these oppositions stem in part from a social order, and a conception of society, that we have already moved somewhat beyond. Conceived as antagonistic ways of explaining and dealing with sex hierarchy, the conflicts between separation and social participation, and between the claims of sex on the one hand, and race and class on the other, are themselves expressions of the nineteenth-century conception of two sociosexual spheres. It is this conception that feminist social theory is at the point of overcoming—not by suppressing such oppositions, but by understanding the systematic connections between them.

Superimposing the Spheres

One of the new and striking features of contemporary feminist thought, and of the objectives of the women's movement, is how, despite such tensions, certain differences are being superseded. In thought and practice, neat distinctions we once made between sex and class, family and society, reproduction and production, even between women and men seem not to fit the social reality with which we are coping.[11]

Studies such as Adrienne Rich's on the institutionalizing of motherhood, and those of Dorothy Dinnerstein and Nancy Chodorow on the psychic and social effects of female care of infants, demonstrate how sexual/reproductive arrangements, for example, shape men as well as women—as fathers and husbands, and also as policymakers, as the male gender in whatever role. Those arrangements, societal as well as affective in origin, shape public life and policy in the very attitudes toward nature, life, and power borne by the gender that must overcome the Mother. Similar to this appreciation of the public import of personal relations, is our recognition of the role of social agencies in the childrearing once ascribed to women and private families. In addition to families—and even assuming many of their former functions—nurseries, daycare centers, schools, and the media all participate in the so-called domestic work of social reproduction.[12] And finally, just as the entire economy and society works to reproduce itself, so we have come to realize that women produce, and always have produced, goods and services for society at large as well as for their families. Woman the gatherer may have sustained hunting-gathering societies even more than man the hunter did, and in every age women as well as men have engaged in the basic production of their societies.[13]

These new perceptions are emerging out of a newly complex social experience. With more of the work originally done at home becoming socially organized, and women following their work into the domain of socially organized production, women in increasing numbers are living in both the woman's and the man's world. We are living in the sphere of the family and of social production, and as we do so, we become increasingly aware of how the social relations arising from each sphere structure experience in the other. To be a mother in one domain deeply affects one's position, tasks, and rewards in the other domain. Mothering determines where and at what hours women work, and thus the jobs for which they are available. Conversely, the inferior pay and benefits of women's work in a sex-segregated labor market perpetuate women's economic dependence upon men. They pressure women to form sexual and/or familial attachments to men; and in the family ensure that the man's position will determine the place of residence and the unbalanced allotment of responsibility for domestic work and childcare to women.

Experiences such as these increasingly make us aware that *woman's place is not a separate sphere or domain of existence but a position within social existence generally.* It is a subordinate position, and it supports our social institutions at the same time that it serves and services men. Woman's place is to do women's work—at home and in the labor force. And it is to experience sex hierarchy—in work relations and personal ones, in our public and our private lives. Hence our analyses, regardless of the

tradition they originate in, increasingly treat the family in relation to society; treat sexual and reproductive experience in terms
of political economy; and treat productive relations of class in
connection with sex hierarchy.[14]

In establishing these connections, feminist thought is moving
beyond the split vision of social reality it inherited from the recent past. Our actual vantage point has shifted, giving rise to a
new consciousness of women's "place" in family and society.
From today's more advanced social situation, what we see are
not two spheres of social reality, but two (or three) sets of social
relations. For now, I would call them relations of work and sex
(or class and race, and sex/gender). In a Marxist analysis, they
would be termed relations of production, reproduction, and
consumption. In either case, they are seen as socially formed relations. They are seen to obtain for women and men, and to do
so *at the same time* in any particular experience—be that work or
leisure, familial or social, personal or public. Relations of work
and sex (or production, reproduction, and consumption) affect
women and men differently, making "women" and "men" social
categories, just as worker and bourgeois are, and black and
white. Relations of work and sex combine so as to give women
and men different relative positions in society and the family,
different powers, hence different sexual, affective, and social experience. And such relations also affect women differently by
race and class. Thus female sexuality is subject to male control
by the welfare relation as well as by the marital one. Class and
race determine access to contraception and abortion on the one
hand, and sterilization on the other.[15] And similarly, with regard
to work and class position, women's subordinate position in the
sex/gender system is expressed in super-exploited sex-typed
jobs for the majority, but also in the discriminatory pay and advancement of more privileged women who do find equal work.

From this perspective, our personal, social, and historical experience is seen to be shaped by *the simultaneous operation* of relations of work and sex, relations that are systematically bound to
each other—and always have been so bound. That is, we are
moving beyond a nineteenth-century conception of society because our actual vantage point has shifted. But just as the earth
and planets revolved around the sun long before Copernicus

"saw" that those were the relations of the solar system, so this dialectical (or relational) unifying of our vision of the social order gives us a sounder basis for understanding society—even society of the nineteenth and early twentieth centuries. The conception of two social spheres existing side by side simply masked this more complex social reality. It did not describe the society in which it arose so much as reflect it ideologically. Wittingly or unwittingly, it served to legitimate certain of the bourgeois patriarchal practices of that society. At worst, by separating women out of production and making them "the Sex," it drew a veil of Motherhood over the forms of women's oppression that bourgeois society intensified: the economic super-exploitation of working women; gross abuse of the sexual advantage this gave middle-class men; subordination of bourgeois women to the property and personal interests of men of their class; and subjection of women to the demand for ever-increasing population to meet the needs of war and production.

Even in feminist and socialist thought, formed in opposition to capitalism and patriarchy, the theoretical outlook of two sociosexual spheres led to partial theories of social change, and to partial theories of women's oppression and liberation. From today's position, we have already begun to see how earlier feminist and socialist thought itself partakes of the bourgeois and patriarchal outlook insofar as it subscribes to the dualities that society established.[16] We can no longer focus upon productive relations of class, suppressing those of consumption (sexuality/family) as Marx did, or focus on sex and familial arrangements (Freud, and Juliet Mitchell in *Psychoanalysis and Feminism*) without those of class, any more than we can place one sex in the category of sexuality/family and the other in that of society. To do so violates our social experience and the new consciousness that is emerging out of it. A more complex pattern of sociosexual arrangements is called for—and is appearing in feminist social thought. Feminist thought regards the sexual/familial organization of society as integral to any conception of social structure or social change. And conversely, it sees the relation of the sexes as formed by both socioeconomic and sexual-familial structures *in their systematic connectedness*.

The current political goals of the women's movement also indicate how the earlier, split vision of bourgeois patriarchal society is fading. These goals are neither to participate as equals in man's world, nor to restore to woman's realm and values their dignity and worth. Conceptions such as these are superseded in the present will to extirpate gender and sex hierarchy altogether, and with them all forms of domination.[17] To aim at this, as almost all parties (at least within the women's movement in the United States) now seem to do, is to make a program out of the essential feminist perception, that the personal is political. It is a program that penetrates both to the core of self and to the heart, or heartless center, of the male domain, for it will require a restructuring of all social institutions to change our subjective experience in this way. To restructure how we come to know self and others in our birthing, growing up, loving and working, feminist politics must reach the institutions that fatefully bear upon sexuality, family, and community. Schools and all socializing agencies will have to be rid of sex and sexual bias. Work and welfare will have to be transformed, placed in the humane context of the basic right of all to live, work, and love in dignity. And there will have to be genuine participation by all in shaping the modes and purposes of our labor and distributing its returns. A feminist politics that aims at abolishing all forms of hierarchy so as to restructure personal relations as relations among peers has to reach and transform the social organization of work, property, and power.

The theoretical outlook is just forming in which these several relations between sex and society will be examined. Feminist social thought is just beginning to overcome the dualisms it inherited; to account satisfactorily for sex, class, and race oppositions within a unified social theory. It is difficult, therefore, to describe this project clearly, because we are not yet in a position to look back and reflect upon a development that is not yet completed. Yet there is no doubt that most contemporary feminist thought adopts such a unified social outlook; and even at this early stage, certain consequences can be seen to flow from the redirection of thought it entails. I should like to conclude by mentioning three of them.

(1) Understanding women in such systematically unified terms should resolve those conflicts in feminist theory and practice

that result from attempts to reduce sex oppression to class interests, or to see the relation of the sexes as always and ever the
same, regardless of race, class, or society. Oppositions of this
kind are no longer possible in a view that acknowledges the
combined power of sexual-familial and productive relations in
our lives, and the fact that these relations serve male and socioeconomic interests at one and the same time.

That is, a sharpened sense of particularity results from this
vantage point; but the perspective itself unifies what is at once
an economically and a sexually based social reality. Just as we
see women and men in this perspective experiencing work and
personal situations differently because of their respective sex (or
gender) position, so women, because of our different class and
race positions, experience sex oppression differently. The relation of the sexes operates in accordance with, and through, socioeconomic structures, as well as sex/gender ones. Hence, it operates differently in every society, and in the class and racial
groupings of each.

(2) This unified view should enable us to understand better
the persistence of patriarchy. In any of the historical forms that
patriarchal society takes (feudal, capitalist, socialist, etc.), a sex/
gender system and a system of productive relations operate simultaneously. They operate simultaneously to reproduce the socioeconomic and male-dominant structures of that particular
social order. The labors of women that support societal life and
foster its values are thereby perennially harnessed to sustain
and reproduce male dominance. And to men oppressed by the
organization of labor and maldistribution of social wealth and
power in society after society, the dual order of patriarchal society provides in many (but not all) instances the satisfaction of
dominion over women.

(3) While our social understanding becomes more complex
as the earlier, split vision of society merges into this unified,
"doubled" view, the fact that we have such a view indicates that
we are in a new social and political position with regard to patriarchy. It has been a strength of patriarchy in all its historic
forms to assimilate itself so perfectly to socioeconomic, political,
and cultural structures as to be virtually invisible. It could even
couch demands for female subordination in terms of the prevail-

ing social and cultural values: Athenian civilization, bourgeois equality (separate but equal), socialist priority of class struggle. If we are now in a position to see—as I believe we are now seeing—how the sexual/reproductive and the economic productive/reproductive orders operate together, our historical moment must be such that there is no longer that perfect mesh between the two that allowed us to see only one order or the other, but never the combined operation of the two. We must be at some distance from a social order that made one sphere, and one set of relations, fade from view as we looked at the other, so that at best we could establish only a few of the social connections between them. Now, conscious of women's subordinate place in the "private" (sexual/reproductive) and "public" (socio-economic) domain; conscious of how relations of production, reproduction, and consumption operate to make women, as well as men, support a patriarchal social order; ours may be an historical moment when those relations are in sufficient conflict for us not only to "see" how the patriarchal system works, but also to act with that vision—so as to put an end to it.

Notes

1. Juliet Mitchell's article, "Women: The Longest Revolution," first appeared in 1966 in *The New Left Review*, no. 40. She revised it somewhat and incorporated it in her first book, *Woman's Estate* (New York: Vintage, 1973).

2. What follows is not a comprehensive list, but rather examples of contemporary Marxist-Feminist analyses of women's work, in the home and in the work force: Charnie Guettel, *Marxism and Feminism* (Toronto: Canadian Women's Educational Press, 1974), and Dorothy E. Smith, *Feminism & Marxism—A Place to Begin, A Way to Go* (Vancouver: New Star Books, 1977), for general statements of position. For the special analyses of domestic labor and women's work, Margaret Bentson, "The Political Economy of Women's Liberation," *Monthly Review* 24, no. 1 (September 1969); Mariarosa dalla Costa, *The Power of Women and the Subversion of the Community* (Bristol: Falling Wall Press, 1972); the English studies in *The New Left Review* (particularly Jean Gardiner in no. 89 [January–February 1975], "The Role of Domestic Labour"); the United States studies by Lise Vogel, "The Earthly Family," *Radical America* 7 (July–October 1973); and the issues of *Radical America* on women's work (7, nos. 4 and 5 [July–October 1973], 8, no. 4 [July–August 1974]; as well as the three issues of URPE's *Review of Radical Political Economics* on women (July 1972, Spring 1976, Fall 1977). The finest synthesis of much of this thinking is Sheila Rowbotham's *Woman's Consciousness, Man's World* (Middlesex, England: Pelican, 1973). All these studies are contemporary but find

their forerunner in Mary Inman, *The Two Forms of Production under Capitalism* (Long Beach, Calif.: Mary Inman, P.O. Box 507, Long Beach, Calif. 90801, 1964), originally in the *Daily People's World*, 1939.

3. Outstanding examples are Adrienne Rich, *Of Woman Born* (New York: W. W. Norton & Company, 1976), Mary Daly, *Beyond God the Father* (Boston: Beacon Press, 1973), Shulamith Firestone, *The Dialectic of Sex*, rev. ed. (New York: Bantam, 1971), Dorothy Dinnerstein, *The Mermaid and the Minotaur* (New York: Harper & Row, 1977).

4. There are several historical studies of this development. See, e.g., Nancy Cott, *The Bonds of Womanhood: "Woman's Sphere" in New England, 1780–1835* (New Haven: Yale University Press, 1977).

5. "When . . . we ask why the existence of one-half the species should be merely ancillary to that of the other . . . the only reason which can be given is, that men like it." Harriet Taylor Mill, "Enfranchisement of Women" (1851), in John Stuart Mill and Harriet Taylor Mill, *Essays on Sex Equality*, ed. Alice Rossi (Chicago: University of Chicago Press, 1970), p. 107.

6. Because of her sensitivity to sex discrimination in the work force, she was one of the few women committed to the labor movement and socialism who was an active advocate of the Equal Rights Amendment; and, although a socialist and probably a communist in the 1920s, she saw "the woman's battle as distinct in its objects and different in its methods from the workers' battle for industrial freedom." "Now We Can Begin," in *Crystal Eastman on Woman & Revolution*, ed. Blanche Wiesen Cook (Oxford: Oxford University Press, 1978), p. 53 *et passim*.

7. E.g., ". . . the economic dominance of man over woman which long ago led to her dependency and subjection, does not exist any longer for the modern proletarian. The consequences in other spheres which also flowed from that dependency are now obviated." Henriette Roland-Holst, "Feminism, Working Women, and Social Democracy" (1903), reprinted in *Green Mountain Quarterly*, no. 2 (February 1976): 24. Sometimes called the Dutch Rosa Luxemburg, Roland-Holst was a leading Marxist at roughly the same time Crystal Eastman was active, although she lived until 1952.

8. Linda Gordon, *Woman's Body, Woman's Right: A Social History of Birth Control in America* (New York: Viking, 1976), p. 114 *et passim*.

9. Ibid., pp. 240–44.

10. For the ways race, class, and sex (including heterosexist) oppression are experienced in their combination, and the need for a theoretical position that will respect each and encompass all, see Audre Lorde, "Scratching the Surface: Some Notes on Barriers to Woman and Loving," *The Black Scholar* 9, no. 7 (April 1978): 31–35; Barbara Smith, "Toward a Black Feminist Criticism," *Radical Teacher*, no. 7 (March 1978): 20–27; and "The Combahee River Collective: A Black Feminist Statement," in *Capitalist Patriarchy and the Case for Socialist Feminism*, ed. Zillah Eisenstein (New York: Monthly Review Press, 1978), pp. 362–72.

11. For new work systematically connecting sex and class analysis, see Zillah Eisenstein, "Developing a Theory of Capitalist Patriarchy and Socialist Feminism" and "Some Notes on the Relations of Capitalist Patriarchy," in *Capitalist Patriarchy*, ed. Eisenstein. For connection between family, sex, and society, Eli Zaretsky, *Capitalism, the Family, and Personal Life* (San Francisco: Agenda Publish-

ing Co., 1973); Gayle Rubin, "The Traffic in Women: Notes on the 'Political Economy' of Sex," in *Toward an Anthropology of Women*, ed. Rayna Rapp Reiter (New York: Monthly Review Press, 1975), pp. 157–210, and Rayna Rapp, "Family and Class in Contemporary America: Notes Toward an Understanding of Ideology," *Science and Society* 42, no. 3 (Fall 1978): 278–300. For systematic and historical connections between production and reproduction, Linda Gordon, *Woman's Body, Woman's Right*, and for the social/psychic formation of gender, male and female, the works by Dinnerstein and Rich in n. 3 above, and Nancy Chodorow's several studies which have now led to *The Reproduction of Mothering: Psychoanalysis and the Sociology of Gender* (Berkeley: University of California Press, 1978).

12. Renate Bridenthal, "The Dialectics of Production and Reproduction," in *Conceptual Frameworks for Studying Women's History* (Bronxville, N.Y.: Sarah Lawrence Publications, 1975). Rosalind Petchesky and Kate Ellis, "Children of the Corporate Dream: An Analysis of Daycare as a Political Issue under Capitalism," *Socialist Revolution* 2, no. 6 (November–December 1972): 8–28.

13. Traditional Marxist thought regards the relations of production, reproduction, and consumption as forming one systematic social totality. Reproduction is not a separate "mode" of activity; it *is* the social process of production viewed "as a connected whole, and as flowing on with incessant renewal" (*Capital* I, chap. 23). Hence for Marxists, the idea of reproduction includes the notion of procreation and socialization, but applies to the reproducing of the productive system as well. It was chiefly the Frankfurt School and Wilhelm Reich in the twenties who began to work out the distinctive role of the family and sexuality in this reproductive work. Contemporary Marxist-Feminist analysis (in n. 2 above) distinguished women's work within the family. The role of "women's work" in the productive system as a whole has been worked out in the studies by Jean Gardiner, Batya Weinbaum and Amy Bridges, and Heidi Hartmann in *Capitalist Patriarchy*, ed., Eisenstein, and for hunter/gatherer societies by Sally Slocum, "Woman the Gatherer" in *Toward an Anthropology of Women*, ed., R. Rapp Reiter, pp. 36–50; Jane Lancaster, "Carrying and Sharing in Human Evolution," *Human Nature* 1, no. 2 (February 1978): 82–89; Adrienne Zihlmann, "Women in Evolution, part 2: Subsistence and Social Organization among Early Hominids," *Signs* 3, no. 4 (Fall 1978): 4–20.

14. On the old model of separate spheres, and the new one see Rosalind Petchesky, "Dissolving the Hyphen: A Report on Marxist-Feminist Groups, 1–5" in *Capitalist Patriarchy*, ed., Eisenstein, pp. 373–90. All the contemporary works cited in notes 10–13 above—and many others not cited here—are establishing these connections.

15. *Workbook on Sterilization and Sterilization Abuse* (Bronxville, N.Y.: Sarah Lawrence Publications, 1978); Helen Rodriguez-Trias, M.D., "Sterilization Abuse," *Reid Lectures* (New York: Barnard College, 1976).

16. It was in critiquing Juliet Mitchell that this became especially evident. See Eli Zaretsky, "Male Supremacy and the Unconscious," *Socialist Revolution*, nos. 21–22 (January 1975).

17. Two major exponents of this view (and there are many, many others) are Mary Daly and Sheila Rowbotham, nn. 1 and 2 above.

FOUR

Early Feminist Theory and the *Querelle des Femmes*, 1400–1789

W e generally think of feminism, and certainly of feminist theory, as rising in the nineteenth and twentieth centuries. Most Anglo-American studies of the
women's movement acknowledge some "forerunners" in the English and French Revolutions and in
individual figures such as Anne Hutchinson, but only
with Seneca Falls does a continuously developing
body of feminist thought seem to emerge. Histories
of French feminism claim a longer past. They tend to
identify Christine de Pisan (1364–1430?) as the first to
hold modern feminist views, and they survey other
early figures who expressed pro-woman ideas from
Christine down to the French Revolution.[1] Even in
this literature, the sense of a theoretical feminist tra-

I am grateful to the National Endowment for the Humanities for
funding the research for this paper as part of a larger study of the
history of feminist thought, and to Christina Greene for her invalu-
able work as my research assistant.

An earlier version of this paper appeared in *Signs: Journal of
Women in Culture and Society* 8, no. 1 (Autumn 1982): 4–28. It was
also presented at a conference on power and authority in the
seventeenth-century, Reid Hall, Paris, and was discussed at the Columbia University Seminar on Women and Society. I am indebted
to participants at both meetings for many helpful suggestions. Particular thanks go to Bonnie Anderson, Adrienne Block, Blanche W.
Cook, Clare Coss, Moira Ferguson, Martin Fleisher, Patricia Gartenberg, Danielle Haasc-Dubosc, Allison Heisch, Abby Kleinbaum,
Claudia Koonz, Gerda Lerner, Rosalind Petchesky, Catharine
Stimpson, Amy Swerdlow, Paula Wiggins, and Marilyn Young.

dition predating the revolution is obscured. Feminist women scarcely appear in most books on feminist thought in early modern French and English literature.[2] When they do, they and their ideas seem isolated, separated from each other and from us by long periods of silence and inactivity.

New work is now appearing that will give a fuller sense of the richness, coherence, and continuity of early feminist thought. I should like this paper to contribute to that end.[3] I hope to demonstrate a solid, four-hundred-year-old tradition of women thinking about women and sexual politics in European society before the French Revolution. Feminist theorizing arose in the fifteenth century in intimate association with, and in reaction to, the new secular culture of the modern European state. It was the voice of literate women who felt themselves and all women maligned and newly oppressed by that culture, but who were, at the same time, empowered by it to speak out in women's defense. Christine de Pisan was the first such feminist thinker, and the four-century-long debate on women that she sparked, known as the *querelle des femmes*, became the vehicle through which most early feminist thinking evolved.

The early feminists did not use the term, of course. If they had applied any name to themselves, it would have been something like "defenders" or "advocates" of women, but it is fair to call this long line of pro-women writers that runs from Christine de Pisan to Mary Wollstonecraft by the name we use for their nineteenth- and twentieth-century descendents. Latter-day feminism still incorporates the basic positions the feminists of the *querelle* were first to take. Because these positions belong to a general vantage point these women won and secured, I prefer to call them "positions" rather than ideas proper. They define an outlook within which ideas develop, a "theory" in the original sense of the term, a conceptual vision.[4] That theory was essentially oppositional to the dominant culture in three specific ways:

1. The *querelle* is almost all polemical.[5] From Christine de Pisan on, women's defenses of women were responses to specific, published attacks upon them. Their educational writings were equally, if indirectly, polemical, for they had had to argue against cultural and social constraints on women that published attacks justified. In all these writings, women took a conscious, dialecti-

cal stand in opposition to male defamation and subjection of women.

2. In their opposition, the early feminists focused upon what we would now call gender.[6] That is, they had a sure sense that the sexes are culturally, not just biologically, formed. Women were a *social* group. They directed their ideas against the notions of an inherently defective sex that flowed from the misogynous side of the debate, and against the societal shaping of women to fit those notions.

3. The immediate aim of these feminist theorists was to oppose the mistreatment of women. Their concern was for women, that they might have the knowledge and confidence to reject misogynist claims. But their understanding of misogyny and gender led many feminists to a more universalist outlook than the accepted value systems of the time allowed. By exposing ideology, and opposing the prejudice and narrowness it fostered, they stood for a general conception of humanity.

The ideas of the early feminists bear the marks of their social and intellectual climate, of course. Early modern Europe was in the process of state formation. Princely rule, rank, and hierarchy coexisted with bourgeois modes of life and work and with a developing republican (liberal) ethos. On one hand, feminist theory was both shaped by the new pressures this society created for women and stimulated by its possibilities. On the other hand, aristocratic women lost considerable economic, political, and cultural power as compared, not only to their feudal forebears, but to men of their own class. At the same time, a class of women emerged, shaped by a new gender construction of the domestic lady. The contents of early feminist theory reflect the declining power of women of rank and the enforced domestication of middle-class women. Yet it owes its very being to new powers of education some of these women had at their command.

To think of their privileged, literate culture as a determining factor indicates the barrier of class that separated the feminist theorists of the *querelle* from social action. Their history resembles that of early socialism in this regard. Both were responsive to the new society of early modern Europe, to its possibilities and abuses. But in feminism, as in socialism, theorists such as Christine de Pisan and Thomas More, Lucrezia Marinella and Tommaso Campanella, Mary Astell and the Abbe Morelly had few or no connections with the movements for social change that periodically erupted and were suppressed. Such movements were isolated and/or short lived, confined to classes of people whose powers were not yet fed by the productive forces of the age. It would take the French Revolution and the industrialization of Europe and North America before social theory and practice would cohere, bound by democratic movements that were broad enough to aim at transforming the entire structure of hierarchical society.

To be sure, the Beguines of the late medieval cities were also certainly "feminist" in the sense given above, as opposing misogyny and male subjection of women. These were celibate lay women who sought to live in their own communities, and to support themselves by their collective work. Taking only temporary religious vows, they escaped two of the major institutions of male power: the family and the Church. Social acceptance was another matter, however, and when state and Church combined to crush the movement, they succeeded.[7] Nonetheless, the will to independence from male authority was clearly present with the Beguines.

It was also present during the revolutionary days of the English sects. In the 1630s and 1650s, many of the radical sects supported religious equality for women. In this climate, in which it was acceptable to assail patriarchal rule in general, there were women who actively liberated themselves from male clerical authority and their husbands as well. They sought to control their own consciences, to preach, and to improve women's educational and economic opportunities.[8] They, like Anne Hutchinson, their counterpart in seventeenth-century New England, I would call "feminists in action" rather than theorists.[9] Rather than elaborating their ideas in writing, they used them to modify or organize social forms in which women might be free of male power and authority over them. Their heirs are the women of the French and nineteenth-century revolutionary movements, and of the successive phases of the nineteenth- and twentieth-century women's movement. Feminist activity by that time found its voice in literate, theoretical reflection; and theory, in turn, sank roots in a movement of women for democratic change. Then, but only then, could feminist theory be ordered along political lines. Only as theory found a new basis in social action could it advance ideas of social reorganization.

Until that time, when a women's movement joined feminist theory and practice, the early feminist theorists carried on their long and patient intellectual resistance at a remove from action. The struggle of the *querelle* was carried on mostly by the female members of a distinctively modern, literate class that served the upper reaches of a ranked society or, less often, by women of those higher ranks. In the main, they were the forebears of what Virginia Woolf called "the daughters of educated men" [10]— daughters in revolt against the fathers who schooled some of them for a society they forbade all women to enter.

1. The *Querelle* Commences

If Petrarch can be called the first modern man, then Christine de Pisan, the poet and author who introduced her countrymen, Petrarch and Boccaccio, to Parisian culture in the early 1400s, is surely the first modern woman. Petrarch's consciousness is what has made him seem "modern" to historians, literary critics, and biographers. [11] His self-consciousness arose from social, rather than mystical experience, and from republican, rather than a feudal, social outlook.

Psychologically rather than spiritually self-aware, ambitious, concerned with his social image, with success and lasting fame, despite his profound Christian convictions, steeped in the language and literature of "pagan" antiquity, his response to classical culture was as prophetic as it was nostalgic. He appears in the condensing lens of history as the first master of a literary mode of learning, and of a direct prose style, that could once again serve civil society and purposes of state. Looking to his social origins, we see Petrarch somewhat more accurately as expressing, as well as shaping, the outlook of an entire class of urban and courtly literati. Clerics becoming humanists, they, like he, were the Latin secretaries of princes, lay and clerical, and of republics. They assumed the new offices of state. They became the tutors and educators of those who would govern and those who would surround the governing classes as Europe moved out of feudalism.

This professional class strode onto the stage of modern history, as did the business families they largely derived from. Many of the feminist writers—Aphra Behn, Mary Astell, and the Venetian poet Lucrezia Marinella—had solid merchant fathers or husbands. Many more were the sisters, daughters, and nieces of humanists and teachers and were educated by them. Rachel Speght was probably educated by her schoolteacher father, Mary Astell by her clergyman uncle. Bathsua Makin, Judith Drake, and Elizabeth Elstob were the sisters of Oxbridge fellows and shared in their learning. Christine, a humanist by profession, had been married to a royal secretary. Educated in French and Italian literature and some Latin by her Italian father, a councillor and physician at the Valois court, she decided to support herself, her children, and her widowed mother as a copyist and author when she was widowed at the age of twenty-five. She studied throughout her life and turned out some fifteen volumes of work in seventy large notebooks. Most of her work was widely diffused, bringing her both fame and subsidies.

Despite this, Christine suffered a variety of humiliations in attending the royal court on her own behalf, having to brave whistles and shouts on the streets as well as in the palace. She was crossing a line between private and public life that was to be drawn with increasing firmness for middle-class, and even noble, women. Indeed, none of the feminists who followed her were to lead so independent and public a life until the seventeenth-century dramatist, Aphra Behn, herself unusual for her time. However, even to share in private the learning and outlook of their humanist relations and teachers had a dramatic effect on such women. Sharing meant discovering that the seemingly universal ideal of *humanitas* the new learning fostered, the notion of education as cultivating the human in man,[12] was not meant for "man" male and female, anymore than the occupations of the literati were. In short, no sooner had a humanistic outlook started to form among the upper reaches of lay society and among its authors and teachers, than a fateful dialectic began between its female and male proponents.

Imbued with renascent ideas of civic virtue, humanism was unhappily far more narrow in its views of women than traditional Christian culture had been. The religious conception of women, although misogynist in its own way, did regard them as equally capable of the highest states "man" could attain: salvation and sainthood. Classical republican thought, rooted in a society that confined women to a *gynecaeum* and reserved political life for men, threw in doubt this sense of a single human destiny—or even a single human nature. As Boccaccio said of almost all the illustrious women he commemorated in his *De claris mulieribus* (1355–59), "What can we think except that it was an error of nature to give female sex to a body which had been endowed by God with a magnificent virile spirit?"[13] Only as viragos, as exceptions to their sex, could women aspire to the Renaissance ideal of "man."[14]

Beginning in 1399, Christine wrote a series of works in which she set herself up as a defender of her sex, to criticize and rebut the sharp turn toward misogyny in the attitudes and the reading of her time. For a woman to talk back to ribaldry and misogyny was new, in writing at least, in the language of literature and learning. Christine was fully aware of the novelty of her position. She wondered, in *The City of Women* (1404), her major "defence" of women, why women had not taken up their pens before, to protest the vile things written and said about them. Three visionary Ladies who inspired Christine to do so assured her, however, that this task was destined for her, among all other women. She was to be the first to have the "new thought" to write on "what might be the cause . . . that so many different men, clerics and others, . . . think and write so much slander and such blame of women and their condition." And by so doing, she would construct "a cloister of defence," a book that would be a citadel, fortified by such arguments that women of all stations might there withstand the assault of their male attackers.[15]

Christine's opposition to misogyny gave rise to the four-century-long debate on women concerning their evil and their excellence; their equality, superiority, and inferiority to men; and, simply, their defense.[16] The themes of the *querelle* arose earlier than 1400, and they persisted beyond 1789, yet these dates mark unmistakable turning points in its history. The century before Christine knew several kinds of literature on love, marriage, and women. The courtly tradition was generally pro-women in the sense of chivalric, but there was also a clerical

tradition and a secular bourgeois one that were decidedly misogynous. By 1400, in the secular (and vernacular) literature of
England and France, the earlier "gentle" attitudes of the court
were losing ground before these *fabliaux* and poems of bourgeois
origin, vigorous and crude in their criticism of nobility, clergy,
and of women, love, and marriage. Jean de Meung's section of
the *Roman de la Rose* (1277) is the classic statement of this kind
of mockery of women and chivalric love. It echoed thirteenth-
century invectives against women and sanctioned them in a
work of undeniable literary merit. The popularity of these works
mounted throughout the fourteenth century. As the *Roman de la
Rose* (which was taken up by Chaucer in England) and the bourgeois satires found imitators of noble, as well as clerical and
bourgeois origins, efforts were made to shore up the waning
spirit of courtesy. In 1399, the knightly Ordre de l'Escu Vert à la
Dame Blanche was founded in France for the defense of
women's interests and honor, and in 1400 the dukes of Bourbon
and Burgundy organized a "Court of Love" for the same purpose, to which Christine belonged. In this context, Christine
wrote her poem of 1399 (*Epitre au Dieu d'Amours*), deploring the
great vogue of the *Roman de la Rose* and the attitudes it promoted
toward women, its reduction of romance to sexual conquest and
abandonment.[17]

This intervention on behalf of women provoked a minor
querelle de la Rose, as it was called: a set of letters and poems in
which Christine was reproached for her daring and her reputa-
tion was called into question. She defended herself and intensified her criticism of de Meung's work as "an exhortation to
vice."[18] Although troubled by the storm she aroused, she was
apparently undaunted, for in 1404 she took on a highly popular
work expressing the other, clerical strain of medieval misogyny,
Les lamentations de Matheolus, written a decade or so after de
Meung's *Romance*, very much in its satiric vein. It is about a
cleric, Mathieu, who marries a widow, and enumerates his complaints about marriage. Christine found Matheolus of little significance as an author, but she was deeply disturbed by the
number of such clerical attacks on women and marriage. Most of
them, as she noted, were meant to dissuade fellow clerics from
marriage and the loss of sinecures they would suffer thereby.
But in addition to their commonplace complaints against the

married life, these works were filled with loathing for women and the female body.[19] Matheolus and the hundreds of other such works he stood for and drew upon, inspired *The City of Women*.

Christine focused on just one issue, the attack on women that these writings contained. Moreover, her defense of women was shaped by a theoretical intention. Unlike the few thirteenth- and fourteenth-century poems, such as *Dit des Femmes* and *Bien des Fames*, that praised women in response to the invectives against them, Christine's "new thought" was to investigate as well as rebut misogyny. Most remarkable, the debate on women that Christine launched would no longer present two male-defined sides of the issue, as had the clerical debate on marriage and the bourgeois satires and responses. Christine had created a space for women to oppose this onslaught of vilification and contempt, and the example of her citadel served them for centuries.[20] Although men continued to write in defense of women, what is novel about the *querelle des femmes* is that women seized upon it to rebut for themselves the misogynist voice of literate opinion.

Developments on the misogynous side of the new and the older debates were nowhere near as dramatic. The position of the clerics and schoolmen on the old debate over the celibate versus the marital state, and the contemplative versus the active life, was overwhelmed by the pro-marriage and pro-family treatises of the humanists and reformers of the fifteenth and sixteenth centuries. But these works were by no means feminist, despite their reconciliation with sexuality. Indeed, the growing acceptance of an active and familial life as the social norm, which accompanied the rise of bourgeois society and the state, fed directly into the new debate on women and accounts for much of its popularity. The "moderns" on the misogynous side of the *querelle des femmes* dropped some (but only some) of the clerical abhorrence of female sexuality and invoked scripture primarily on the issue of woman's subjection to man, now that she was to be wed. Like the Graeco-Roman authors they preferred to draw upon, their intent was not to dissuade anyone from marriage, but to justify woman's confinement to it because of her rational inferiority to them. "Surely all can never be mistaken" runs a typical "learned" diatribe:

> *"Do not all Writers,* [sacred and profane] without comparing
> Notes, combine in painting them false as they are fair, and
> silly as they are sweet; artful in modest Guise, and impudent
> when Lewd; treacherous, ambitious, Slaves to Avarice, the
> Foes of Reason, and Never Friends to Thought. If *Seneca* may
> be believ'd, *'a Woman* never muses by herself, but she is
> musing on some Wickedness.' All are of his Mind, and all
> consider them at best as flattering, pleasing, desirable Evils.
> *Democritus* was so convinced of this, that, being question'd,
> why he who was himself so big had married a Wife so little,
> he answer'd: Methinks, says he, as it is, I have chosen too
> big a one, when all I had to choose was Evil. But Protagoras
> went farther still, no Evil according to him exceeds that Evil,
> Woman. What made him give his Daughter in Marriage to
> his mortal Enemy?[21]

Early modern misogynous literature, despite its modifications of
the medieval tradition, remained as wearisome in its repetitiveness and as obscene in content.[22] The *querelle* served as a progressive and humane purpose only for the defenders of women.

The repetitiveness of the misogynous tradition nonetheless
affected the responses of the pro-woman side. Called again and
again to rebut a flood of arguments to the effect that women
were excluded from the concept of man in scripture, that they
were not truly human, that they were subject to man by the authority of religion and history,[23] the feminists reiterated their
ideas, which in themselves were novel, but did not undergo
much development. The static quality of the genre should not
mislead us into accepting the commonly held notion that the
querelle was a kind of literary game, however.[24]

The misogynists of the *querelle* did not merely hold some contemptuous beliefs about women, or express the central notion of
male supremacy, that is, that woman's chief purpose is to serve
man (or God in him). Most of the male authors regarded as
favoring women did this: Boccaccio, More, and Erasmus, Shakespeare, Montaigne, Locke, Montesquieu, Diderot, Voltaire. The
misogynists, such as Ben Jonson and Alexander Pope, Rabelais,
Boileau, and Moliere, joined the tradition of slanderous criticism
of women as well. An attack on women formed some (or the
only) part of their literary work, and that choice (of which other
men did not avail themselves) is to be remembered when we are

told that such satire was, after all, a literary convention, or that such-and-such an author did depict women favorably else-where. As Rachel Speght responded to one such self-excuser in 1617, "If your own words be true, that you wrote with your hand, but not with your heart, then you are a hypocrite in print: but it is rather to be thought that your pen was the betrayer of the abundance of your mind." [25]

The fact that the women on the feminist side of the *querelle* repeated rather than advanced their ideas has to do with the lack of any underlying social movement to carry their thought forward, as well as with the repetitiveness to which they were responding. However, their personal involvement in those ideas is evident. The engagement of the male authors who followed Christine is more dubious. Their defenses, mostly written for women rulers, are often suspiciously rhetorical in their exces-sive claims for women. Like the widely diffused *De nobilitate et praeccellentia foeminei* (1529) of Cornelius Agrippa of Nettesheim, they invariably claimed that women should exercise every public office, judicial, ecclesiastical, and academic. [26] Moreover, many of the male authors who defended women persuasively set forth the misogynous as well as the pro-woman side of the debate, which makes their concern for women seem at least as literary in origin as it may be heartfelt. Thus, Castiglione gave both sides of the debate in that favored work of Renaissance courtly society, *The Courtier* (1527). Using a bourgeois spokes-man to voice the misogynous part of the dialogue on the Lady, he appears to favor the "gentle" (aristocratic) pro-woman side. Just the opposite is the case with Edward Gosynhill who initi-ated the debate in England. His sentiments clearly lie with his castigation of the argumentative, loud mouthed, gossiping, lazy, greedy, inconstant, immoral, and disagreeable nature of women in *The Schole house of Women* (1541), which went through four editions by 1572, rather than with his own rebuttal, *The prayse of all women, called Mulierum Pean* (c. 1542), which enjoyed no such popularity. [27]

At most, women described opinions they were refuting. They never wrote on both sides of the *querelle* (except for the un-known Sophia of the eighteenth century, and she, if she was a woman, was paraphrasing a male defense that incorporated the commonplace attacks, Poulain de la Barre's 1673 *De l'Egalité des deux sexes*).[28] Indeed, most of their defenses were written, not as spontaneous literary works, but as angry retorts to specific misogynous attacks, as Christine responded to *The Romance of the Rose* and Matheolus's *Lamentations*. Marie de Romieu, stung by a satire written by her brother and determined to prove that women could indeed write, published in 1591 her first poetic work, a discourse on the excellence of women.[29] A number of well-identified English women published such rejoinders, as well as some pseudonymous authors who are clearly women.[30] Three women took up woman's defense in response to a particularly scurrilous pamphlet of 1615: the poet Rachel Speght and two very sharp, seemingly higher placed women who styled themselves Ester Sowernam and Constantia Munda.[31] Joseph Swetnam's *The Araignment of Lewde, Idle, Froward and Unconstant Women* had provoked them by its crude craving for power over women and gross projections. This self-styled "bear-baiter" of women (incoherently) wrote, for example:

> It is not strange of . . . a woman's tongue that neither correction can chastise nor fair means quiet, for there is a kind of venom in it, that neither by fair means nor foul they are to be ruled: all beasts by man are made tame, but a woman's tongue will never be tame.[32]

Swetnam's obsessive contempt for his mother, and his projection of male sexual urges on to "lustful" women, were not lost on his feminist critics, any more than his ignorance of the sources he falsely cited and misquoted. They deftly exposed his illiteracy and illogic. Ester Sowernam (like virtually every feminist in the long debate) had once again to point out how rare it is for women to allure and offer themselves to men, how common for men "to seek and solicit women to lewdness."[33] But if they refuted Swetnam's arraignment easily because of its patent fallacies, his women critics nonetheless felt besieged by "every pedantic goose quill; every fantastic poetaster." Constantia Munda and the circle of women with whom she says she discussed the matter, were clearly outraged by a mounting wave of misogyny streaming from "the scribbling pens of savage and uncouth Monsters."[34]

At the end of the seventeenth century, two English women

felt compelled to reply to "a rude and disingenuous discourse delivered by Mr. John Sprint in a Sermon at a Wedding," which he subsequently published and in which he expounded on the utter subordination of women to their husbands. Eugenia, one of these authors, is not known except as one who "never came yet within the clutches of a husband."[35] The other, the anonymous author of *The Ladies Defence*, was identified in a later edition as the poet, Lady Mary Chudleigh (1656–1710)—one who was married indeed and recommended that women "shun that wretched state."[36]

Another poet, Sarah Fyge Field Egerton, appears to have written *The Female Advocate* (1686)—at age 14!—in reply to the "late satire on women" quoted above (note 22) for its obscenity; Judith Drake penned *An Essay in Defence of the Female Sex* (1696); and women of low and high station continued the polemic in the eighteenth century. A laundress, Mary Collier, who had been taught to read by her parents composed a long poem, *The Woman's Labour* (1739), to refute one Stephen Duck who wrote *The Thresher's Labour* as if only men worked; and Anne Howard, Viscountess Irwin, denounced Alexander Pope's coarse and malicious *Epistle II, To a Lady* at about the same time.[37]

In Italy, Laura Terracina objected in 1555 to Ariosto's portrayal of women.[38] Moderata Fonte wrote a poem on the equality of the sexes; and in 1600, the Venetian poet, Lucrezia Marinella, critiqued the anti-woman sentiments of several of the poets and writers of the Italian Renaissance and refuted general misogynous arguments as well.[39] Marinella even took on male writings in praise of women. She faulted Sperone's dialogue *On the Dignity of Women* (1542) for placing women in a servile relation to men and Tasso's defense of women because he exempted only "heroic women" (i.e., women rulers) from the notion of women's native imperfection.[40]

Many other women joined the fray.[41] If they were not stirred to polemic by particular attacks on their sex, they wrote to counter a general attitude of disdain such as Mlle de Gournay complained of. She, who had been a respected intellectual companion of Montaigne, knew that men would not even read what she had written and that they would boast of it; that no matter how eloquently or well she reasoned, she would be dismissed with that certain nod of the head that means, "it's only a woman speaking."[42] Contempt for women was public and unashamed down through the eighteenth century, when the historian Catherine Macaulay wrote of the "censure and ridicule" women suffer from

> writers of all descriptions, from the deep thinking philosopher to the man of . . . gallantry, who, by the bye, sometimes distinguishes himself by qualities which are not greatly superior to those he despises in women. Nor can I better illustrate the truth of this observation than by . . . the polite and gallant Chesterfield. 'Women,' says his lordship, 'are only children of a larger growth. . . . A man of sense only trifles with them, plays with them, humors and flatters them, as he does an engaging child; but he neither consults them, nor trusts them in serious matters.'[43]

The *querelle* persisted in opposition to this open, published disdain, ringing with the language of battle for four hundred years.

"Our pens shall throttle you . . . we will . . . bait thee at thy own stake and beat thee at thine own weapon," vowed one of the women provoked by Swetnam, the "baiter of women" in 1615. And young Rachel Speght, "armed with the truth," set about her "combat" with Swetnam because as yet she found no other "of our sex to enter the lists."[44] The defenses were "bastions," "sanctuaries," "protections" for women in the fifteenth and sixteenth centuries, titles that follow Christine's notion of a citadel, becoming "ladies' defences" and "female advocates" in the parliamentary climate of the late seventeenth and eighteenth centuries. The genre remained popular through the eighteenth century. In France, Mme de Galien, Marie Armande Jeanne Gacon-Defour, and Mme de Coicy (later author of *Démande des Femmes aux États Genereaux*) all wrote defenses in the spirit of Christine (or of Poulain de la Barre).[45] At the end of the eighteenth century, Mary Ann Radcliffe continued to use one of the favorite titles of the *querelle* in *The Female Advocate* (1799), and Mary Hays and Mary Wollstonecraft were still partly writing in its responsive, polemic tradition.[46]

By the late eighteenth century, however, a new radical content had begun to transform the thematic concerns of the old debate. Mary Radcliffe's plea for working women and prostitutes, Mary Hays's and Mary Wollstonecraft's belief in equal sexual status, as well as equal citizenship with men, broached the economic,

political, and sexual issues of the impending women's movement. Although still reactive to misogyny, the feminists affected
by the French Revolution felt themselves part of a new and
hopeful future for women. They were animated by a notion of
progress and of intentional social change. The feminists of the
querelle were reacting to changes they seemed to have no control
over, or to a Puritan revolution that served mainly to confirm
their subjection to men. Lacking a vision of social movement to
change events, their concern lay with consciousness. By their
pens, they could at least counteract the psychological consequences of what they felt was a recent, steady decline in the
position of women.

2. Consciousness and Culture

To this day, every feminist who has followed Christine de
Pisan has had to pass through the particular crisis of consciousness she described with as much self-awareness as Petrarch
brought to his inner struggles with a dawning modern ethos.
Unlike the early humanist, however, Christine could not draw
upon classical learning to guide her toward her new intellectual
position. She had to oppose what seemed, and still seems to
be, the overwhelming authority of the learned about women's
inferiority.

The force of male disdain for women, not just in this book or
that, but in virtually all the philosophers, poets, and men of
letters (rhetoricians) she read seemed too overwhelming at first
for her to question its objective grounds. It was "too much [to
hold], that so many famous men . . . should have lied, and in so
many places, for I could scarcely find a volume [of moral phi-
losophy], whoever its author, without . . . some chapters or sections blaming of [women]."

Having taken up the issue of misogyny, Christine had begun
to explore women's experience. "I began to examine myself and
my condition," she wrote, "as a woman." She turned to other
women, "to princesses, great ladies, and to gentle women of
lower station in great numbers, all of whom told me freely of
their private and frank thoughts that I might know by my judgment . . . if it were true what so many men . . . witnessed." But
before these first efforts at consciousness raising took hold,

Christine internalized the learned disparagements of her sex. "I relied more on the judgment of others than on that I felt or knew of myself." Out of touch with the ground of truth, her own and other women's experience, she was overcome by men's contempt for women. More and more authors came to mind who found her and all women "abominable," "the vessel, as the men say, of all evil and of all vices." Plunged into sorrow, this first feminist theorist found herself "despising myself and all womankind," assailing her maker because she had not been "born into this world . . . masculine." [47]

Out of this distinctively female anguish, woman's version of the self-disdain of the colonized, Christine's prayer for herself and all women was answered. The allegorical Ladies appeared to her (Reason, Righteousness, and Justice), along with Mary herself. The Queen of Heaven assured her, "I am and shall be evermore the head of womankind." [48] Strengthened by their support, and by the women who spoke to her across class lines of their sense of themselves as women, Christine de Pisan reached what has come down to us as the first analysis of the sexual bias of culture itself. From acceptance of women's inferiority, she moved toward a recognition of the man-made, misogynous nature of that claim. Universal as it might seem, the disparagement of women was not validated by her own and other women's experience. "Although you have seen such things in writing, you have not seen them with your eyes," one of her Ladies pointed out. She had been blinded by those renowned authors into believing "the contrary to that which thou feelest not, nor see not, nor know other than by a plurality of strange opinions." Rather than objective descriptions of female nature and behavior, she now saw the opinions that had immobilized her as projections of men—of male fears, interests, and concerns: "the books that so sayeth women made them not." [49]

Ovid turned from erotic poetry to vicious attacks on women, for example, because, as one of her Ladies informed her, he was castrated. So punished for loving unwisely once too often, he subsequently wanted women to appear unattractive rather than unavailable. The Tuscan poet, Ceco d'Ascoli, defamed women because he had been shunned by them. Moreover, he was burned at the stake for what Christine discreetly referred to as "his vice." [50] Grasping the presence of ideology in what she read, in the form of an ideology of sex, put Christine in a position to critique the image of women she had at first internalized. Her visionary Ladies spoke to her not only in tones of modern empiricism, urging her to accept as true only what conformed to her (and other women's) experience; they also pointed out that the writings of the literate and the learned were distorted by what we now call sexism.

The early feminists took book learning as their starting point, as Christine and the humanists had. Texts, sacred and profane, constituted learning. But the feminists, with no great educational credentials, were unremittingly critical of the authors—ancient, modern, even scriptural—at a time when the *auctores* were still *auctoritates* to many. The explanations they gave for the hostility and bias they found in the traditional texts, and in the "grave dons, learned men, and men of sense" who were writing contemporary invectives against women, [51] were largely psychological, as were Christine's. They particularly noted male competitiveness, how men denigrated women out of fear that women might be found equal, or even superior to them. [52] The Dutch scholar, Anna Maria van Schurman, pleaded with the author of a treatise on women's excellence not to dedicate it to her because of the envy notice of her learning would arouse. "You are not ignorant with what evil eyes the greatest part of men (. . . men of great esteem) do behold what tends to our praise," she wrote in words all the feminists echo. "They think we are well dealt with, if we obtain pardon for aspiring to these higher studies." [53]

The need to feel superior, and displaced sexual feelings, made up a good part of the psychology of educated men. The most systematic analysis of "the causes that impel knowledgeable and learned men to criticize and vituperate women" came from Lucrezia Marinella. She isolated four such causes, three of which (self-love, envy, and their own lack of talent) had to do with a male need to feel superior to women, and one of which (disdain) stemmed from frustration of male sexual impulses. [54] Even Aristotle—or especially Aristotle, because of the authority of his views on women—had to be looked at in his personal sexual relations if those views were to be understood. At times, it was his own sex he loved *con troppo fervore*, Lucrezia Marinella found, leading him to inconsistent, contemptuous statements about women. But also shame, anger, and envy of how women are loved, in particular his feelings towards the concubine whom he married and to whom he was sexually enslaved, led him to deprecate women.[55]

Although they lacked a social analysis of male psychology, the realization that the received wisdom about women stemmed from particular psychosexual experiences, all of them male, gave feminists a critical perspective on the intellectual tradition that was, as far as I can see, unique. The *querelle* as a genre fostered a critical attitude, of course. There were "sides" to the debate on women. Yet only the feminist side refuted texts and authors. Holy Writ and the pithy sayings of the learned were trotted out by all the misogynists, no matter how learned or ignorant they themselves might be. They, and the authorities they cited, attacked women. Feminists attacked, not men, but misogyny and male bias in the literate culture. "We do not menace the men, but their minds, not their persons, but their pens . . . which indeed toward us have been insupportable and intolerable."[56]

Every learned tradition was subject to feminist critique, since all were dominated by men and justified male subjection of women. Feminist wit penetrated to the core of male pretension in the irrefutable arguments and commonsensical adages that supported men's power over women. Strength of mind certainly goes along with strength of body, Mary Astell concurred, "and 'tis only for some odd accidents, which philosophers have not yet thought worth while to enquire into, that the sturdiest porter is not the wisest man."[57] Aristotelians were held up to ridicule for their phallic conception of women as a mutilated or impotent male.[58] If women appeared as "imperfect men" to Aristotle, doubtless that was because "they are deficient in that ornament of the chin, a beard—what else [could he mean]?"[59] but deeper than wit, the feminists saw that the learning they inherited was not merely biased, but deeply flawed by male interest in maintaining the supremacy of men. Mary Astell despaired of learning anything about women from books, "because the writers, being men, envious of the good works of women, haven't recounted their great deeds."[60] The women noted that male authors appealed to Nature and Reason to "explain" the exclusion of women from learning, government, and public office, but we "ought to have better proofs . . . than the bare word of the persons who advance [such arguments], as their being *parties* so immediately concerned must render all they say of this kind highly suspicious."[61]

3. Women and Power

The defenses of the *querelle* then rest upon a refutation of male authority as expressed in what was accepted as knowledge, or learning. That left, as the burden of their response to "those fine discourses which have been made against the women from our great fore-fathers to the present,"[62] recovery of a true image of women—an image that could be safely internalized, to mobilize women's powers.

Initiating what we can call the first attempts at "women's studies," *The City of Women* and the defenses that followed it aimed to reorganize knowledge of women (and men) from a feminist standpoint. As a genre, they consist largely of reinterpretations of the record on women, historical and scriptural. Their rewriting of history, which is what I want to focus on here, is telling for the kind of revisions early feminists wanted to make. The defenses generally spend some time on exemplars of the virtues of women: their chastity, constancy, their labors, all of which were being deprecated. But chiefly, they were concerned with two aspects of women's behavior under special attack. The contempt for women that marked early modern misogyny stemmed from attitudes that accepted, even required, marriage. To reduce women to subjection to husbands, however, and to deny them any other mode of life, women had to be, and were, regarded as rationally defective. They could not govern, nor could they be learned—and exactly those two groups of women, women rulers and learned women, were the ones the early feminists sought in the past. They used history mainly to find precedents for women's governance (and hence their right to self-rule) and for their learning (of which they felt newly and unjustly deprived). Arms and letters, *ars et mars*: women were being shut out of this twofold work of culture and civilization (as upper-class society conceived it) and were told their "nature" did not allow of it. "Would to God," Lucrezia Marinella protested,

> that in our times women were allowed the practice of arms and letters. What marvels would we see. . . . I wish that these [detractors of women] would make this experiment: that they raise a boy and a girl of the same age, and both of sound mind and body, in letters and in arms. They would see in a short time how the girl would be more perfectly instructed than the boy and would soon surpass him."[63]

Short of such social experimentation, what the feminists could and did do was show by historical example what the nature of women really was with respect to power and to reason. Shaped by this objective, the historical content of the defenses is fairly primitive. Like Christine, the feminists simply drew upon the histories of illustrious women that began with Boccaccio, and upon similar ancient and medieval sources, for "examples" of women's capacities.[64] The concept of ideology and gender underlying this work, however, was novel and advanced. Histories are "perverted to debase us," as Sophia maintained.[65] They are "writ by [men]," as Mary Astell put it, and "they recount each other's great exploits, and have always done so."[66] To understand that histories are construed from a male position—and reinforce that position—is a concept not yet accepted by most professional historians. The early feminists were fully aware of such falsification, but to undo its consequences, they thought they merely had to disentangle the truth about women from those same historical sources. "When one is apprised of this inequitable proceeding of the men, and takes the trouble of examining into past times, it appears . . . that the women have not been behind hand with the men in any thing, and that the virtue they have demonstrated upon every occasion is far beyond aught the men can cite in their favor."[67] Christine, casting out all of Boccaccio's notions of the manly and "exceptional" character of women's historic achievements, used his biographies to validate a wholly positive notion of woman's nature.[68] Indeed, she even turned his tales of Isis, Ceres, Minerva, and Carmenta (founder of Rome and the Latin language) into a compelling case for the female origins of culture and civilization.[69]

These mythic founders of language, agriculture, the several arts and sciences and of states dropped out from most later defenses—along with Christine's saints and holy women. Those who remained to figure most significantly as models of womanly nature were women of learning (whom we shall treat elsewhere) and women warriors and rulers. The Amazons were praised century after century for their warlike independence from men, but also for their statescraft.[70] French authors such as Christine and Marie de Gournay celebrated Joan of Arc as warrior—Marie de Gournay expressly classifying her with the Amazons.[71] English women, such as Ester Sowernam, recalled Boadicea, queen of the Britons, who taught the Romans (and the rest of us) "that a woman could conquer them who had conquered almost all the men of the then known world."[72] The defenses commemorate women rulers of antiquity: Queen Semiramis of Babylonia, Zenobia, Hellenistic queen of the Palmyrians, and so forth. They record more recent rulers as well. Christine (who was a historian and did an official history of the reign of Charles V of France) listed the queens of France in *The City of Women*.[73] She noted that some governed in their own right, such as Fredegonde, widow of the Frankish Chilperic; others, like Queen Blanche, were regents. Ester Sowernam did the same for England. The Saxon queens, Elfgive and Edith, were rulers and conquerors; queens from Norman times to the Tudors ruled as wives and mothers but then came Elizabeth, "the glory of our sex, a pattern for the best men to imitate."[74]

To Christine, the Salic Law (1328), removing women from inheritance of the French crown, was still new and offensive. She noted that the reigns of the queens of France were just and moderate and that the same could still be said of many women, "great ladies, modest, and lesser ones," who sustain and direct territory their husbands governed during their lifetime and who are just as greatly loved by their subjects.[75] Women were still governing and defending domains in Christine's lifetime. She herself wrote a book on warfare, and she required ladies in her *Livre des Trois Vertus* to know how to command, in defense and attack.[76] However, as the European states consolidated, women were steadily excluded from such functions. As the military, financial, and juridical powers of feudal families became "public," that is, state functions, men moved into the new positions of

state control—and the male conception of ladylike behavior assumed its more modern form. Castiglione, who transformed the
feudal lord into a courtier, defining his style of life for generations of Europeans who henceforth served a prince, defined the
lady's new mode as well. Still "courteous" toward ladies, he
granted them equal learning with the courtier. But contrary
even to contemporary practice, he removed them from training
at arms and horsemanship.

In Castiglione's lifetime, Eleanor of Aragon, as duchess of Ferrara, assumed sole command of the city when it was besieged by
Venice in the war of 1482–84, and Caterina Sforza ruled her
petty state of Pesaro in her own name, taking command and
fighting to maintain it. Indeed, as we are now beginning to re-
discover, women were a normal part of European armies from
the fourteenth until well into the nineteenth centuries, in addition to the noblewomen who participated in positions of command.[77] Nonetheless, by the second half of the seventeenth century, Castiglione's image of the disarmed lady, excluded from
functions of state, prevailed throughout Europe as ideology—
and increasingly as reality. "All heroic actions, public employ-
ments, powerful governments, and eloquent pleadings are
denied our sex in this age," Margaret Cavendish wrote in 1656,
under Commonwealth rule. Her words remained as true for
Restoration as for republican England. Although duchess of
Newcastle, as exceptional for her intelligence as for her connections, she had to settle for writing as the only outlet for her ambition. She would not even read history, she claimed, certain as
she was of how different it was for women in the past where she
would find "such of my sex that have outdone all the glory I can
aim at."[78]

In the face of such changes in the power of women, the feminists of the *querelle* developed another strategy to fight back.
They used that surety about the valor, martial ability, and government of women in the past to make their point: that women's
powers, and the prevailing notion of woman's nature, were
newly restricted. Marie de Gournay noted rightly that the Salic
Law was devised to control a disputed succession: it was enforced only in France, and even there, women in earlier times
had as great a deliberative role as men. In the remote past, the

Spartans consulted with their women on all "public and private" matters, as did the Germans of Tacitus, and other nations were ruled only by women.[79] The spinsters Mary Tattle-well and Joane Hit-him-Home raised the ghost of the crudely armed Long Meg of Westminster to do battle for her sex in *The Women's Sharpe Revenge*. Meg had earned King Henry's praise for the good fight she showed the French at the Battle of Boulogne (1544): "with my blows and knocks, I made their bones ache." Now her memory was evoked to protest the seventeenth-century belittlement of women.[80] The feminists rightly understood that the issue of female power was critical, even for women of no rank. Something more was at stake than the participation of upper-class women in the exercise of state functions. The notion was forming that women *as women* were devoid of power and authority by their very nature. This, indeed, was what the *querelle* was largely about. On the feminist side, Amazonian figures and tales of matriarchy, along with biographies of actual women warriors and rulers, were perpetuated to keep alive a fading image of independent women and of women as makers of culture and civilization.

On the misogynist side, men of otherwise opposed classes and parties were joining ranks in a newfound conviction about woman's "natural" subjection to man.[81] Republicans, bourgeois by class and outlook (as in Renaissance Florence and Venice, Calvinist Geneva and Puritan England), had no question about the domestic and subordinate nature of women.[82] From Geneva, John Knox's *The First Blast of the Trumpet against the Monstrous Regiment of Women* (1558) heralded God's word on how monstrous it was for a woman to reign over men. Banished from England and Scotland by Mary Tudor and the regent Mary of Guise, Knox had his own personal and political reasons to storm at governance by women. But his position was validated in the public eye by two major developments that were affecting women in the process of state formation. One was the loss of power women of rank suffered as states eroded the military, juridical, and political powers of aristocratic families. The other was the formation of the preindustrial, patriarchal household as the basic social unit, as well as the economic unit of postfeudal society. State legislation in the fifteenth and sixteenth centuries strengthened the household as an instrument of social control. Poor laws, laws against vagrants, prostitutes, witches, even against religious orders in Protestant countries, herded people into households for their livelihood and placed unpropertied males—and all women—under the governance of the house-hold "master." [83]

Even Elizabeth's accession later in 1558 did little to fortify the older traditions of female rule. Her reign stilled any further blasts from Knox's trumpet, but not the precedence that pre-rogatives of sex now took over rank. John Aylmer, who refuted Knox when Elizabeth was already queen (he was subsequently made bishop of London), contended in his semiofficial defense of female power that "a woman may rule in her capacity as a magistrate and yet obey as a wife." [84] Elizabeth's government was not to have any bearing on women as a sex. "Vertuous women wisely understand," Spenser assured Elizabethan England,

> That they were born to base humilitie,
> Unless the heavens them lift to lawful soveraintie. [85]

Indeed, if anyone sought to assimilate herself to the Renaissance notion of the virago, it was Elizabeth—the virginal, "honorary male." As queen, she gave no indication in her manner or deeds that other women could excel in any way. Her propaganda re-ferred consistently to her ability to rule as "an exception to the Law of Nature," whereas her sex was a matter of frailty and modesty, as in her famous Tilbury speech: "I know I have the body of a weak and feeble woman, but I have the heart and stomach of a king, and of a King of England too." [86]

However, as the feminists of the *querelle* pointed out, women had not always been regarded as weak and feeble, because they had not been so. Indeed, strong measures had been taken to force them into that mold. After Elizabeth's "exceptional" reign, James I of England initiated a little known statist phase of the *querelle* by imposing such measures—demonstrating that not only republicans or Puritans, but staunch upholders of rank and monarchy were now to deny women any semblance of political or military power. James had as domestic a view of women as any bourgeois. When presented with a young woman famed for her knowledge of Latin, Greek, and Hebrew, his response was, "But can she spin?"[87] Nor could Knox out-do James's revulsion to female power. His advice to his eldest son on his marriage was: "Ye are the head, she is your body. It is your office to command, and hers to obey."[88] This conception of women's role he imposed on aristocratic women, in a remarkable drive to force them to give up such familiar prerogatives as the wearing of riding attire and the use of weaponry.[89]

James's campaign began in January 1620, when he ordered the bishop of London to instruct all clergy "to inveigh vehemently against the insolencies of our women, and their wearing of broad brimmed hats, pointed doublets, their hair cut short or shorne, and some of them stilettoes or poniards."[90] The modern gender requirements for ladies, such as Castiglione had set forth, were now to be enforced by fiat: passing down the hierarchy from king to bishop to all clergy. Culture, too, was officially enlisted to support state and Church.[91] Poems, plays, ballads, sermons, and pamphlets warned women to desist from the offending modes of dress and behavior now designated as "masculine."

Three pamphlets of 1620 make particularly clear how the bourgeois domestic norm was being extended to all women, and how right the feminists were to sense that the battle of the sexes conducted by way of the *querelle* was a battle over gender: over how women were to be perceived—and to be. *Hic Mulier* began the attack on women who were "masculine in their gender," as its title also indicates by gender crossing (as in *le femme*). What was perceived as masculine was exactly the free and dashing costume James had condemned, along with short hair and wearing of weapons.[92] At just about this time, the Puritan, William Prynne, was also objecting to the "whorishness" of short hair. Like "wearing the breeches" in the family, cropped hair threatened a significant aspect of the godly social order, namely, the power relation of the sexes which it seemed to symbolize. Was not hair women's "natural veil . . . the very badge and character of their subjection both to God and Man?"[93] Philip Stubbes, a Puritan pamphleteer of the 1580s, wrote similarly of the denigration of "godly, sober women in wearing a wanton kind of attire proper only to men," and he was certain such women who adopted men's fashions would as soon become men if they could.[94] The tracts stemming from the king's campaign had nothing to do with Puritan propriety, of course. Nowhere do they criticize the dress of other ladies of fashion which fully exposed their breasts, for example.[95] It was clearly the independence of "masculine" women, or their parity with men, that was threatening and subjected them to attack.[96] Their easy riding attire, short hair, and particularly their weapons, masculinized them, made them "man in body by attire, man in behavior by rude complement, man in nature by aptness to anger, man in action by pursuing revenge, man in wearing weapons, man in using weapons."[97]

Although the monarchs of early modern Europe were all moving to disarm their nobility at this time, and to tame them to state rule, upper-class women were being additionally tamed to male familial and social rule, as the Jacobean gender debate shows. *Haec Vir* (like *la homme*), a second pamphlet that appeared the week after *Hic Mulier*, seems to promote a certain parity between women and men in the gender controversy, because it also urges men not to be effeminate. It offers some veiled criticism of James's openly homosexual court, of the curled and powdered hair, affected speech, makeup, and recreations of his courtiers. Yet men are promised that if they become masculine again, women will be "beautiful" and "serve" them. Masculine women and effeminate men should both change dress and restore the natural order—but that order (even for James's notorious court) closely approximates Puritan notions as far as women were concerned. Subjected by (hetero)sexiness, sewing, and scripture, they would wear "hats to defend the sun, not to cover shorne locks . . . shaped, comely and close gowns, not light skirts and French doublets, for poniards, samplers, for pistols, prayer-books, and for ruffled boots and spurs, neat shoes and clean gartered stockings."[98]

The third pamphlet in this series stepped up the patriarchal theme. In the moralistic tones of the middle-class critic, the author reduced the entire issue of gender and cross-dressing to the paternal authority of the bourgeois family. "A woman was created to honor her parents [read father] and obey her husband," he wrote;

fathers to use their lawful authority over their children; husbands to overrule and command their wives: as he therefore is an effeminate man that transfers his birthright upon his daughter or wife, so is she a masculine woman that bereaves parents of authority, husbands of supremacy, or debords from the modesty required in her sex.[99]

The shift in tone and conception from James's pronunciamentos on the "poniards, pistols and the ruffling yellow" of aristocratic women, to the third of the pamphlets on masculine women, presaged a social upheaval soon to affect crown, Church, and aristocracy—but not women. When the Puritan Revolution overthrew the royal hierarchy, the domesticated bourgeois woman became the indisputable norm for English society. The effects of the bourgeois construction of gender were already evident in Elizabeth's public stance as virago, however, as they were in the Jacobean gender controversy. Even *Hic Mulier*, which is quite aristocratic in its focus, proposed the bourgeois curb of economic dependency for independent women. If the fathers, husbands, or sustainers of the "hermaphrodites" would but close their liberal hands, or demand a strict account of what they gave for their maintenance, they were assured the women's "excesses" would soon cease.[100] James's measures to control women would soon be as archaic as his views on the divine right of kings. He had availed himself of direct royal power in his contest with English ladies over their dress. When he had a Mrs. Anne Turner executed in 1615 on a charge of poisoning, he required that she (and the hangmen) wear another item of dress that had offended him, a starched yellow ruff which she had popularized as a fashion for ladies. In 1620 he had the Church, the theater, pamphleteers, ballad makers, and singers all join in vilifying as "masculine" the women who rode in easy costume and armed themselves. Notoriously hostile to women's independence and power, he sought to subdue them to his notion of "the modest woman."[101]

Despite the social reality that removed all women but queens from the direct exercise of power by the late seventeenth and eighteenth centuries, the historical memory of armed women and female government persisted in the defense of the *querelle*. The other theme in the gender controversy—that of women's learning—became the more vital one, but queens and possible queens continued to stir feminists by their mere being. They also gave material support to the feminists' efforts to break through the barrier of women's presumed ignorance and incapacity, as did other women in high places. Christine de Pisan had written her book on the education of women for Margaret of Burgundy as she was about to marry the French dauphin; Bathsua Makin wrote hers for Mary, eldest daughter of the duke of York. Astell directed her proposal for a woman's college to the future Queen Anne, then princess of Denmark (who indeed intended to subsidize it, until the bishop of Salisbury dissuaded her).[102] Marie de Gournay dedicated her *Egalité des Hommes et des Femmes* to Anne of Austria, then queen of France, and was pensioned by her as by her predecessor, Marie de Medici. Lady Chudleigh, who authored *The Ladies Defence*, dedicated her poems to Queen Anne and her essays to the Electress Sophia.[103]

The most telling example of how female power continued to inspire the feminist side of the *querelle* is to be found in Mary Astell. Astell did not write a defense, but, in addition to her well-known proposal for a women's college, she wrote a stunning critique of marriage.[104] Subscribing to the principles of the Anglican church and a ranked society, she described husbands in the first edition of this book in the hierarchical terms of early modern society. They were "lords and masters" of their wives who were but "poor vassals."[105] Astell was tempted by the liberal position of John Locke on the right to revolt against tyranny, but only to the point of questioning how husbands should govern. Rank, including the superior rank of husbands, and the right of superiors to rule their inferiors seemed providential: "God has placed different ranks in the world, put some in a higher, and some in a lower station . . . for many good reasons." It was not a good enough argument for Astell herself, however, that superiors "from the throne to the private family" ruled as representatives of God. She did not marry and could not advocate it for women. But then Queen Anne came to the English throne in 1702. A woman was governing in her own right once again, and this precipitated in Astell a fascinating feminist version of the enlightened revolution in thought.

This High Church woman, who objected in print to Locke's

deistic views, now adopted one of the major arguments that freed scientific thought from the hold of scripture and the Church. In a 1703 appendix to her *Reflections on Marriage*, she invoked the principle Galileo had used to defend the movement of the earth around the sun. Arguing that scriptural language conforms to custom so as to better convey its unique theological message, she dismissed biblical references to women's subjection as but another such accommodation to prevailing ways. The relation of the sexes is a universal issue, she found. It pertains to human nature at large, not just to the recipients of Revelation. The equality of women was therefore an issue for Reason to decide—and clearly, with Anne governing England, all the evidence of sense and reason argued against male superiority. Not only was every man not superior to every woman; one woman was now superior to every man in the realm. If every woman were subject to any man by some Law of Nature, Astell pointed out, the queen would have to obey her footman. And if men were now to fall back from that position, maintaining that women's inferiority means only that some women are inferior to some men, well that is no more true than its reverse: that some men are decidedly inferior to some women.[106] So much for the presumed natural inferiority of women. The old principle of female rule had once again won out over the doctrine of woman's universal subjection to man.

The power of women of rank was a weak foundation on which to rest hopes for woman's ultimate emancipation, as Astell did.[107] By the beginning of the eighteenth century, their sway had been sorely limited, as the feminists themselves had been noting, and by the end of the century, rank itself was to be swept away by the bourgeois social order. Yet in the historical transition from feudal to bourgeois society, most of the early feminists of the *querelle* continued to appeal to, and carried on a conservative romance with, female representatives of the old order. In part, their political conservatism was a limitation of their class. Isolated by class privilege from most other women, they had little knowledge of their lives and did not look to them as a source of power. For all their fierce retorts to misogyny, for example, they never noticed its single most horrendous expression in early modern Europe, the hanging or burning alive of some 100,000 or more women as witches. Like the early modern utopian socialists, whom they resemble in this regard, the early feminist theorists looked to enlightenment and the traditional sources of power when they hoped for social change. Because they were women for whom sexual politics were central, they looked with nostalgia to times when those traditional powers were exercised by women.

Even their sexual politics appear conservative to our time. What the feminists of the *querelle* had to say to women and society was largely reactive to what the misogynists said. Yet the way beyond that resistance to misogyny had to lie through it. The alternative was to accept and internalize the images that showed women of all ranks their inferiority and subjection to men. To oppose misogyny was to initiate a long feminist struggle. The greatest achievement of the early feminist theorists was to set that dialectic in motion. They were limited to a battle of pens, but in that battle they exposed the male bias of learning and its misogynous intent. And they won, at least for feminist consciousness, a broader and more generous view of women than the narrowing gender prescriptions imposed by early modern society.

These gains were never lost. During the centuries when the powers of aristocratic women became ever more restricted, and law, economics, and public authority restrained those of middling and poorer women from breaking forth into public life, the feminists of the *querelle* defied and denied the accompanying images of women that robbed them of dignity and authority. They rejected as male ideology the ideas of women's incapacity that reflected and reinforced the systematic transfer of power and authority to men. And they thereby created an intellectual tradition in which the memory of the feudal rule of women, and dimmer memories of women armed and warring, kept alive a notion of woman's native powers.

As yet no one knows the full extent and effectiveness of that tradition.[108] It is clear that feminist writers drew strength and arguments from their predecessors. Their tradition went beyond the *querelle*. The concern of early feminism with male ideology and gender has remained central to subsequent feminist thought. Despite later developments in consciousness, even their historical record of women warriors and rulers has appeared and reappeared, from Harriet Taylor Mill in the beginning of the first wave of the women's movement to Mary Beard at its end, and it still functions as an empowering image in the semimythical descendants of the defenses, such as Helen Diner's *Mothers and Amazons* (1929) and Elizabeth Gould Davis's *The First Sex* (1971).[109] Beyond the bounds of theory we can only speculate on what the counterculture imagery of the early feminists inspired. We do know, however, that when women rose to join the revolution that put an end to feudalism, they were once again women who armed themselves and sought public power. They formed military units they called Amazon Legions, and they demanded political rights for women—albeit as citizens, this time, not ladies.[110]

Such, then, were the contributions of early feminist theory. The women of the *querelle* initiated and carried on a four-century-long tradition of intellectual opposition to misogyny. They showed how learning was used to belittle women and they created a countervailing image of historic female power. The power of woman's mind they defended with just as much vigor. Letters, as well as arms, formed their twofold "defence" against the misogynous use of culture.

Notes

1. Léon Abensour, *Histoire générale du féminisme* (1921; Geneva: Slatkine Reprints, 1979). This is actually a history of French feminism. Also, Abensour, *La femme et le féminisme avant la revolution* (Paris; E. Leroux, 1923); Lula McDowell Richardson, *The Forerunners of Feminism in French Literature of the Renaissance: From Christine of Pisa to Marie de Gournay* (Baltimore: Johns Hopkins University Press, 1929). Notice the early feminists are "forerunners" in this title rather than feminists in their own right.

For the Anglo-American tradition, I am referring to the orientation implicit and sometimes explicit in most monographic work rather than to general historical accounts of feminism, but Eleanor Flexner's *Century of Struggle: The Woman's Rights Movement in the United States* (New York: Atheneum, 1970) is a good example of such a general account for American feminism. The soundest, indeed the sole, general history of feminism is Sheila Rowbotham's *Women, Resistance, and Revolution: A History of Women and Revolution in the Modern World* (New York: Vintage Books, 1974). As she says, however, this is a history of women coming "to revolutionary consciousness"; it is not a history of feminist theory per se and by definition does not linger over early feminist thought which predates or lies outside the revolutionary tradition.

2. This is the literature on the *querelle des femmes* cited below, n. 16.

3. Moira Ferguson's *First Feminists: British Women Writers from 1578–1799* (Old Westbury, N.Y.: Feminist Press, forthcoming) is pre-eminent among such works for giving a sense of the abundance of feminist writing in the early modern period and its continuity, even though she is concerned only with writers in English. I am deeply indebted to Moira Ferguson for the benefit of exciting correspondence and conversations about her work, for her careful editing of my own, and for the use of her unpublished materials, which she generously shared with me. See, too, Hilda Smith, *Reason's Disciples: Seventeenth Century English Feminists* (Urbana: University of Illinois Press, 1982), and Ruth Perry's forthcoming biography of Mary Astell. Other useful sources for early feminist English writings are Patricia Gartenberg and Nena T. Whittemore, "A Checklist of English Women in Print, 1475–1640," *Bulletin of Bibliography and Magazine Notes* 34, no. 1 (January–March, 1977): 1–13, and an as yet unpublished anthology of women's writings of the English Renaissance by Patricia Gartenberg, with an introduction, which she, too, has generously shared with me; Allison Heisch, ed., *English Women in Print, 1475–1700*, partially complete project based at the Huntington Library; Mary R. Mahl and Helene Koon, *The Female Spectator: English Women Writers before 1800* (Old Westbury, N.Y., and Bloomington, Ind.: Feminist Press and Indiana University Press, 1977).

4. The Oxford English Dictionary defined feminism as a state of being feminine or womanly in 1846 and 1892 (*The Compact Edition of the Oxford English Dictionary* 1: 982) as did the 1901 edition of the *Dictionary of Philosophy and Psychology* 1: 311). By 1906, however, the *Dictionnaire de philosophie* defined feminism as a position favorable to the rights of women (p. 521). Ellen DuBois found in her research for *Feminism and Suffrage: The Emergence of an Independent Women's Movement in America, 1848–1869* (Ithaca: Cornell University Press, 1978) that the term "feminism" was in general use around 1910 to describe that political movement, and that that usage originated in France (personal communication). Linda Kealey, writing about Canadian but also U.S. feminism, found the term used by the 1890s to refer to the New Woman. She also notes that recent women's history has refined the term, distinguishing between different strands of feminism (e.g., "maternal feminism"), all of which recognize, however, the right of women to a public role and to define themselves autonomously (*A Not Unreasonable Claim: Women and Reform in Canada, 1880's–1920's* [Toronto: Women's Educational Press, 1979], pp. 6–8.

Such a refinement can already be found in an essay in the 1915 edition of *The New International Encyclopedia* 8: 441–47). This comprehensive and sophisticated article by Juliet Stuart Poyntz holds that the term originated in France about 1890, that it has been used in English since then to describe the ideas at the root of the "modern woman movement" as well as the social processes which give rise to those ideas in their several forms, e.g. socialist feminism, Christian feminism. It locates the origins of feminism in the social forces transforming feudal into modern industrial society and in the current of democratic thought that accompanied that transformation. Christine de Pisan's *Cité des dames* is named as one of the first feminist works, along with several of the books that originated in the *querelle* (although the *querelle* itself is not mentioned). From a systematic point of view, the article gives one formulation of the third of the constitutive ideas of feminism set forth in this paper. The first two are implicit: opposition to misogyny (social and cultural) and an understanding of women as a social group rather than a biological one. The third arises from the author's definition of feminism as standing for the full emancipation of women.

5. Moira Ferguson noted this in "Thinking in Common, or Feminist Polemic: The Repossession of Another Genre for the Women's Literary Tradition," Paper read at MLA, December 30, 1979, San Francisco; also, Introduction to *First Feminists*. Poems, plays, and novels are further sources for feminist ideas, becoming particularly rich in the seventeenth and eighteenth centuries. I use only those that form part of the *querelle*.

6. The standard theoretical definition of gender is by now Gayle Rubin's, who speaks of a "sex/gender system" as that "set of arrangements by which a society transforms biological sexuality into products of human activity, and in which these transformed sexual needs are met." Gender "is a socially imposed division of the sexes . . . a product of the social relations of sexuality" which "transforms males and females into 'men' and 'women'" ("The Traffic in Women," *Toward an Anthropology of Women*, ed. Rayna Reiter Rapp [New York: Monthly Review Press, 1975], pp. 159, 179).

7. The two major factors which led ultimately to the disintegration of Beguinal life were (1) charges of religious heresy and immorality by the Church and, even more important, (2) economic sanctions imposed by both Church and state. Although the Beguines enjoyed ecclesiastical patronage and secular privileges such as special charters, gifts of land, and freedom from certain taxes, such privileges were not unconditional. Numerous statutes attempted to rectify the *privilegia beguinalia* by imposing economic restrictions on the Beguines. (For example, the Liege synod of 1287 explained that such privileges were intended only for Beguines who earned less than ten marks.) Many of the statutes were a direct result of complaints from the guilds, especially the silk spinners and linen and wool weavers, who resented the economic competition of the Beguines. Restrictive ordinances of the fourteenth and fifteenth centuries left the Beguines in a peculiar position: on the one hand, they were expected and encouraged to earn their own livelihood and customarily engaged in such activities as weaving, spinning, carding, sewing, washing, nursing, and teaching children to support themselves. On the other hand, their efforts to become or remain economically self-sufficient were resented and hindered. Their economic position was further aggravated or undermined when charges of heresy justified the seizure of Beguine property by the Church. See Ernest W. McDonnell, *The Beguines and Beghards in Medieval Culture, with Special Emphasis on the Belgian Scene* (New Brunswick, N.J.: Rutgers University Press, 1954). For an interesting, but somewhat romanticized portrayal of medieval Beguinal life, see Gertrude Robinson, "The Beguines: A Study in the Vocations of Uncloistered Women," *Dublin Review* 160 (London, 1917): 215–33. For a more recent study, see Jean Claude Schmitt, *Mort d'une heresie* (Paris, 1978).

8. Rowbotham, *Women, Resistance, and Revolution*, pp. 21–30; Keith Thomas, "Women and the Civil War Sects," *Past and Present* (April 1958): 42–62; Christopher Hill, *The World Turned Upside Down* (New York: Viking Press, 1972), pp. 247–61.

9. Adrienne Rich coined the term to refer to the various forms of women's resistance to male tyranny that are to be found in every culture and period, "often, though not always, without a theory" ("Compulsory Heterosexuality and Lesbian Existence," *Signs* 5, no. 4 [Summer 1980]: 652).

Some of the seventeenth-century sectarians, such as the English Quakers Margaret Fell Fox, Elizabeth Hooton, and Elizabeth Bathurst, are known for their writings as well as their social activity and held decidedly feminist views. I would argue, however, that their feminist ideas still remain in the context and in the service of religious dissent. In general, the early feminist activists promoted causes that subsumed the interests of women, whereas the theorists were animated by a purely feminist cause but did not see how social movement or women at large might promote it.

10. Two notable exceptions to the bourgeois or aristocratic origins of most of the early feminist theorists are the pseudonymous authors, Mary Tattle-well and Joane Hit-him-Home, of *The Women's Sharpe Revenge* (London, 1640) who claim to be spinners (but see below, n. 30, regarding possible male authorship of this work). Also, Mary Collier, who wrote *The Woman's Labour: An Epistle to Mr. Stephen Duck* (London, 1739), was a laundress.

11. Petrarch was "one of the first truly modern men" to Jacob Burckhardt, the doyen of Renaissance historians (*The Civilization of the Renaissance in Italy* [1860; London: Phaidon Press, 1950], p. 179). Also see Pierre de Nolhac, *Petrarque et l'humanisme*, 2 vols. (Paris, 1907). Later assessments found him a transitional figure, conflicted about the modern, secular ideas and attitudes he was experiencing and expressing. See, e.g., Ernst Cassirer, *The Individual and the Cosmos in Renaissance Philosophy* (New York: Harper and Row, 1963), pp. 15, 37–38; Paul Oskar Kristeller, *Eight Philosophers of the Italian Renaissance* (Stanford, Ca.: Stanford University Press, 1964), p. 13: "Petrarch was both medieval and modern, and as he once stated himself, he looked backward and forward at the same time, as if placed at the frontier of two countries."

12. "What the Greeks call 'paideia' we call 'studia humanitatis,' for learning and training in virtue are peculiar to man, therefore our forefathers [the Romans] called them 'Humanitas'" (Battista Guarino, *De ordine docendi et studendi*, in William Harrison Woodward, ed., *Vittorino de Feltre and Other Humanist Educators* (New York: Columbia University, Teachers College, 1963), p. 177. See also Introduction.

13. Boccaccio, *Concerning Famous Women*, translated and with an Introduction by Guido Guarino (New Brunswick, N.J.: Rutgers University Press, 1963), pp. xxxvii, 87, 131, 217.

14. On viragos, see Allison Heisch, "Queen Elizabeth I and the Persistence of Patriarchy," *Feminist Review* (February 1980): 45–56. See also Margaret King, "Thwarted Ambitions: Six Learned Women of the Italian Renaissance," *Soundings: An Interdisciplinary Journal* 59, no. 3 (Fall 1976): 280–304; "The Religious Retreat of Isotta Nogarola (1418–1466)," *Signs* 3, no. 4 (Summer 1978): 807–22; "Book Lined Cells," in Patricia Labalme, ed., *Beyond Their Sex: Learned Women of the European Past* (New York: New York University Press, 1980), pp. 66–90.

15. Christine de Pisan, *The City of Women*, I. 3, 4; II. 53. The original *Livre de la cité des dames* (1404) is unpublished to this day despite its wide diffusion and

effect. I am using the Brian Anslay translation, *The Boke of the Cyte of Ladys* (London, 1521). I have modernized the spelling and where necessary the words of this text, as I have with other early English writings I quote.

The standard biography of Christine is by Marie-Joseph Pinet, *Christine de Pisan, 1364–1430: Étude biographique et littéraire* (Paris, 1927). For a concise contemporary reassessment of her work, see Susan Groag Bell, "Christine de Pizan: Humanism and the Problems of a Studious Woman," *Feminist Studies* 3, nos. 3–4 (Spring/Summer 1976): 173–84. I have not used her correct spelling of Christine's family name because its French version is so familiar, even though it misleads one into thinking she came from Pisa. Also see Rose Rigaud, *Les idées féministes de Christine de Pisan* (Neuchatel: Attinger Frère, 1911).

16. Christine's role is not adequately appreciated in the literature of the *querelle*, primarily because these works concentrate on the male authors. Blanche Hinman Dow did see *The City of Women* as "the point of departure for that literature in defense of women which was to attest the new interest in an old quest," but she gave no reasons for her judgment (*The Varying Attitude toward Women in French Literature of the Fifteenth Century* [New York: Institute of French Studies, 1936], p. 128). Also, Emile Telle noted how Christine reoriented the medieval, clerical debate on marriage to a debate on women; *L'Oeuvre de Marguerite d'Angoulême, Reine de Navarre et la Querelle des Femmes* (Geneva: Slatkine Reprints, 1969), pp. 9–43.

For the early history of the *querelle*, see in addition to the above, Richardson, *Forerunners of Feminism*, and Francis Lee Utley, *The Crooked Rib: An Analytical Index to the Argument about Women in English and Scots Literature to the End of the Year 1568* (Columbus: Ohio State University Press, 1944). Ruth Kelso covers much of the Italian and some of the European and English Renaissance literature in *Doctrine for the Lady of the Renaissance* (Urbana: University of Illinois Press, 1956). For the later English literature, in addition to Ferguson's *First Feminists*, see Carroll Camden, *The Elizabethan Woman* (Houston: Elsevier Press, 1952); *The Cambridge History of English Literature* 3: 99–102; Doris May Stenton, *The English Woman in History* (1956; New York: Schocken Books, 1977), pp. 127–151, 205–8, 292–8. For a superb social analysis of the seventeenth-century *querelle* in France, see Carolyn Lougee, *Le Paradis des Femmes: Women, Salons, and Social Stratification in Seventeenth-Century France* (Princeton: Princeton University Press, 1976). Katharine Rogers, *The Troublesome Helpmate: A History of Misogyny in Literature* (Seattle: University of Washington Press, 1966), covers ancient, medieval, and modern misogyny, and hence a goodly portion of the misogynous side of the debate.

17. Christine de Pisan, *Oeuvres Poétiques*, ed. M. Roy (Paris: Société des Anciens Textes Françaises, 1886–1896), 2: 1–27. Adrienne Block has shown a similar development in French court songs in which chivalric sentiments were supplanted in the fifteenth and sixteenth centuries by coarsely expressed themes of rape and seduction taken over from popular songs ("Images of Women in Sixteenth-Century French Popular Song" manuscript).

18. On the *querelle de la Rose*, see Charles F. Ward, *The Epistles on the Romance of the Rose and Other Documents in the Debate* (Chicago: University of Chicago Press, 1911). Also, Dow, *The Varying Attitude toward Women*, and Richardson, *Forerunners of Feminism*.

19. *Epitre au Dieu d'Amours* in *Oeuvres Poétiques*, 2: 1–27. In a good example of such clerical dissuasions, many of which drew upon Theophrastus' *De nuptiis*, the Florentine humanist, Leon Battista Alberti, wrote: "You can never love her [woman] without bitterness, fear, misfortune, and worry. Malevolent creature, given us by nature in too great abundance, so that no place is free of them; if you love them, they will torment you and enjoy keeping you to themselves, having torn you from yourself and your own spirit." This is a paraphrase of a twelfth-century piece by Walter Map, *Dissuasio Valerii*, in *Leon Battista Alberti: Opere volgari*, ed. C. Grayson. (Bari: Laterza, 1966), 2: 372. Alberti also wrote one of the best-known humanistic treatises in praise of marriage and family, in which classical forms of misogyny augment and reshape the medieval attitudes.

20. It is difficult to assess the extent of Christine's influence until a comprehensive study of the *querelle* is made. However, her arguments and the historical content of *The City of Women* reappear with variations in almost all of the subsequent defenses by female and male authors.

Martin Le Franc cited Christine as an example of women in his very influential *Le Champion des dames* (1440–42). Pierre Monnier de Lesnauderie did the same in *La louange du mariage et des femmes vertueuses* (1534), expressly recommending her *Cité des dames*. Like Christine, Francois de Billon built a "fort" for women, using illustrious women as his "towers," in *Le Fort inexpugnable de l'honneur du sexe féminin* (1555), and he, too, made women the inventors of agriculture, warfare, letters, etc. On these works, see Richardson, *Forerunners of Feminism*, pp. 38–42, 64–65, 90–100. The idea of a citadel or fort also inspired Daniel Tuvil's *Asylum Veneris: or, A Sanctuary for the Ladies* (London, 1616).

21. "Sophia," *Man Superior to Woman*, in *Beauty's Triumph; or, The Superiority of the Fair Sex Invincibly Proved* (London, 1751). This is a piece of feminist literature that incorporates the misogynous commonplaces.

22. On the repetitiveness and malice of such literature, from the Greeks and Romans through the Middle Ages and early modern period (and in the nineteenth and twentieth centuries as well), see Rogers, *The Troublesome Helpmate*. Obscenity abounds in this literature, from authors of renown such as Ben Jonson and Pope to scurrilous pamphleteers such as Joseph Swetnam. To give but one example, after four and a half pages on the whorishness and other crimes of women, the Restoration author, Robert Gould, adds:

> And now, if so much to the World's reveal'd,
> Reflect on the vast Stores that lie conceal'd;
> How, when into their Closets they retire,
> Where flaming Dil[doe]s does inflame desire,
> and gentle Lap-d[ogs] feed the am'rous fire . . .

Then on and on to the inevitable womb, "greedy as the gaping tomb," which takes in "men, dogs, lions, bears, all sorts of stuff,/Yet it will never cry—there is enough" (*Love Given O're* [1682]). This is the satire against women that provoked Sarah Fyge Field Egerton's *The Female Advocate* (1687). Both works are in *Satires on Women*, Augustan Reprint Society, no. 180 (Los Angeles: University of California, 1976).

23. In Gratian du Pont, for example, *Controverses des sexes masculins et femenin* (1534), and Acidalius Valens, *Dissertation paradoxale, où l'on essaye de prouver que les femmes ne sont pas des créatures humaines* (1595). Both of these major works of the *querelle* are summarized in Richardson, *Forerunners of Feminism*, pp. 66–71, 143–45.

24. This is the commonly held view in the literary histories. Emile Telle, for example, did not find any "real" misogyny in the clerical expressions of disgust about women and marriage, nor in the *querelle* (*L'Oeuvre de Marguerite d'Angoulême*). Even a woman scholar of the early *querelle* excused much of its misogyny as "a conventional acquiescence to a popular vogue" and "a literary pose" (Dow, *The Varying Attitude toward Women*, pp. 114, 115). There is no way to argue against this position save to ask what men would think if women turned out a corpus of literature expressing disgust for men and marriage for a couple of centuries, then modified it to a generalized expression of contempt for men for four centuries more. Would that be a "merely literary" matter?

25. Rachel Speght, *A Muzzle for Melastomus* (London, 1617), p. 23.

26. Agrippa presented his *De nobilitate* to Princess Margaret of Austria in 1529, although he had written it some ten years earlier. It was expanded for the Medici court in 1559 by Ludovico Domenichi, and this version in turn was incorporated by William Bercher-Barker in his *Nobylytte of Woman* dedicated to Queen Elizabeth in 1559. In Italy, Eleanor of Aragon, as duchess of Ferrara, attracted an early *De laudibus mulierum* in the 1480s. Werner L. Gundersheimer gives a good summary of the contents and sources of this work in "Bartolommeo Goggio: A Feminist in Renaissance Ferrara," *Renaissance Quarterly* 33, no. 2 (Summer 1980): 175–200. Unfortunately, he does not compare it with Christine's *Cité des dames* to which it seems heavily indebted, except to conclude (incorrectly) that Goggio is more "advanced" in his feminism than she. Tasso did a similar work for the duchess of Mantua, praising her "manly" virtues and those of other women rulers. Queen Anne of Bretagne stimulated several French defenses of women in the early 1550s, including a translation of Boccaccio's book on illustrious women, and Marguerite of Navarre attracted more such works later in the century.

27. On Goyshnhill, see Camden, *The Elizabethan Woman*, pp. 241–71.

28. The three parts of Sophia's work are *Woman Not Inferior to Man* (1739), *Man Superior to Woman* (1739), which refutes the first, and *Woman's Superior Excellence over Man* (1740), which is a very persuasive presentation of that position, argued with wit and passion. The three are bound in *Beauty's Triumph.* (London, 1751).

When Rachel Speght set forth the slanders of Joseph Swetnam so as to respond to them in her *Muzzle for Melastomus* (1617), she was criticized for doing so in two other responses to Swetnam by the feminists "Ester Sowernam" and "Constantia Munda." Patricia Gartenberg has pointed out to me that Speght defended herself against their charges of repeating libels against women in subsequent writings, denying that she had done so.

29. Marie de Romieu, *Brief discours, que l'excellence de la femme surpasse celle de l'homme* (Paris, 1591). See Richardson, *Forerunners of Feminism*, pp. 123–25.

30. Certain pseudonymous rebuttals may be questioned for male authorship, such as the earliest English example, *Jane Anger Her Protection for Women* (Lon-

don, 1589) and *The Women's Sharpe Revenge* of 1640 by the self-styled spinners, Mary Tattle-well and Joane Hit-him-Home. Jane Anger's tract was also a response to a lost pamphlet according to Utley, *The Crooked Rib*, p. 314. The "spinsters" directed their work against John Taylor, "who writ those scandalous Pamphlets, called the Juniper and Crab-tree Lectures."

See Ferguson, *First Feminists*, for bibliography on both works and for Taylor as a possible author of *The Women's Sharpe Revenge*. I have seen only incomplete copies of this work, which break off at page 214. It is clear the author(s?) had some training in Latin, but at the same time, the homely metaphors and roisterous language fit their ostensible class. Jane Anger's name need not be pseudonymous. There were a couple of Jane Angers living at the time, but the case has been made that a male parodist wrote the work, perhaps John Lyly. See Helen Andrews Kahin, "Jane Anger and John Lyly," *Modern Language Quarterly* 8, no. 1 (March 1947): 31–35.

31. Rachel Speght, *A Muzzle for Melastomus* and *Certain Queries to the Baiter of Women* (London, 1617). On her life and work, see *DNB* 18, p. 429, and Ferguson, *First Feminists*.

Ester Sowernam wrote *Ester hath hang'd Haman* (London, 1617) and Constantia Munda did *The Worming of a Mad Dogge* (London, 1617). On the Swetnam controversy, see Camden, *The Elizabethan Woman*, pp. 241–71; Stenton, *The English Woman in History*, pp. 204–8.

32. Joseph Swetnam, *The Araignment of Lewde, Idle, Froward and Inconstant Women* (London, 1615), p. 40. Swetnam's *Araignment* was very popular; it went through twelve editions between 1615 and 1690. A play was even put on in London called *Swetnam the Woman-Hater, Arraigned by Women*, possibly by Thomas Heywood (1620).

33. Ester Sowernam, *Ester hath hang'd Haman*, pp. 44–45.

34. Constantia Munda, *Worming of a Mad Dogge*, pp. 1–5.

35. "Eugenia," *The Female Advocate* (1699). See Stenton, *The English Woman in History*, pp. 204–8.

36. Lady Mary Chudleigh, "To the Ladies," *First Feminists*. Sprint was a nonconformist minister. His sermon was published a year later as *The Bride-Woman's Counsellor* (London, 1700). Lady Chudleigh's response is *The Ladies Defence; or, a Dialogue between Sir John Brute, Sir William Loveall, Melissa, and a Parson* (London, 1700).

37. For excerpts, analysis, and biographical sketches of most of the British feminist authors, see Ferguson, *First Feminists*.

38. Laura Terracina, *Discorse sopra tutti li primi canti d'Orlando Furioso* (1550). See Kelso, *Doctrine for the Lady of the Renaissance*, pp. 5–37.

39. Lucrezia Marinella cites Moderata Fonte's *Il merito delle donne* (1600) several times but rejects her argument for equality in favor of the superiority of woman to men (*La Nobiltà et l'eccellenza delle donne co' diffetti, e mancamenti de gli huomini* [1600; Venetia, 1621]. For a biographical sketch, see *Enciclopedia Biografica e Bibliografica Italiana* 2, ser. 6: 9–10; Antonio Belloni, *Il Seicento: Storia letteraria d'Italia* (Milan: Vallardi, 1958), 9: 198–99.

40. Marinella, *La Nobiltà delle donne*, pp. 161–80.

41. Marguerite of Navarre composed a book of letters "pour défendre son sexe contre d'injuste mépris" which is lost but was summarized in a later work. Gabrielle Suchon's utterly feminist views are set forth in her *Traité de la Morale et de Politique* (Paris, 1693) and, in a work much like Mary Astell's contemporary *Reflections upon Marriage, Du Célibat Volontaire ou la vie sans engagements* (Paris, 1700), in which Suchon advocates a single life for women.

Richardson in *Forerunners of Feminism* and Kelso in *Doctrine for the Lady of the Renaissance* cite as pro-women writers the poet Louise Labé; Hélinsenne de Crenne, author of the first autobiographical novel, for her criticism of her husband's attitudes, *Epistres familiers* (Paris, 1538), Epistre III; Madeleine Des Roches for urging women to write, particularly against their accusers, *Oevres* (1579), "Epistre aux dames, Ode 3"; Charlotte de Brachart for maintaining that men deprive women of education to magnify their own attainments in her *Harengne* of 1604. This latter reference is incomplete, and I have been unable to trace it. There are undoubtedly many other as yet unknown women who joined the *querelle*, some of whom are mentioned in the writings of women we do know.

42. Marie de Gournay, *Grief des Dames* (1676), in *La Fille d'alliance de Montaigne: Marie de Gournay*, ed. Mario Schiff (Paris: Librarie Honore Champion, 1910), pp. 89–91, 94–95. The editor and biographer of Mlle de Gournay, writing in 1910, was still saying, "it's only a woman." He found himself "exclaiming impatiently" with her contemporaries; he confessed, "this girl gives herself the airs of a man!, but ultimately she inspires . . . a certain respect." Not too much respect, however. Professor Schiff felt constrained to point out that the price of Mlle de Gournay's learning was that she knew neither youth nor beauty. She owed her "petite immortalité" to her friendship with Montaigne, rather than to anything she herself accomplished. Even her failings (as we might suspect) did not belong to her personally. In polemic, "*faithful to the tactics of her sex*," she takes feelings for proofs and sympathies for arguments" (ibid., pp. 45, 1, 8, 25; italics are mine).

43. Catherine Macaulay, *Letters on Education* (Dublin, 1740), pp. 130–31.

44. Constantia Munda, *Worming of a Mad Dogge*, p. 16; Speght, *Dedicatory Epistle*.

45. Mme Galien, de Château-Thierry, *Apologie des Dames appuyée sur l'histoire* (Paris, 1737). Marie Armande Jeanne Gacon-Dufour, *Mémoire pour le sexe féminin, contre le sexe masculin* (London, Paris, 1787). Mme de Coicy, *Les Femmes comme il convient de les voir, ou Apperçu de ce que les femmes on été, de ca qu'elles sont, et de ce qu'elles pourroient être* (London and Paris, 1785). See Abensour, *Histoire générale du féminisme*, p. 175.

46. Mary Hays, *Appeal to the Men of Great Britain in Behalf of Women* (1789; New York: Garland Publishing, 1974). Mary Wollstonecraft, *A Vindication of the Rights of Woman* (1792; New York: W. W. Norton and Co., 1967).

47. Christine de Pisan, *The City of Women*, I.1.

48. Ibid., III.1.

49. Ibid., I.2; II.13. No one has surpassed Christine's description of the passage to feminist consciousness until our own day with Mary Daly's powerful formulations, particularly in *Beyond God the Father* (Boston: Beacon Press, 1973), pp. 13–55. Drawing upon the theological, existential tradition, Daly writes of

the movement through doubt and "divided consciousness" to a feminist position, and of the "courage to be" required to hold on to that place "on the boundary" of a male-dominant culture and society.

50. Christine de Pisan, *The City of Women*, I.9, 13.

51. Mary Astell, *Some Reflections upon Marriage, with Additions*, 4th ed. (London, 1730), p. 74.

52. Drake, *An Essay in Defence of the Female Sex*, pp. 20–25; Anna Maria van Schurman, *The Learned Maid; or, Whether a Maid May be a Scholar?* (London, 1659), pp. 23–41; Marinella, *La Nobiltà delle donne*, pp. 181–82; Sophia, *Woman Not Inferior to Man*, p. 28.

53. Schurman, "Letter to John Beverovicius," in *The Learned Maid*, pp. 38–39.

54." Desiderando alcuno di adempire le sue sfrenate voglie, et non potendo per la temperantia, et continentia di quelle, subito si sdegna, et adira: e adirato dice tutti quei mali, che son possibili a ritrovarsi, si come di cosa odiosa, et pessima" (Marinella, *La Nobiltà delle donne*, p. 145).

55. Ibid., pp. 40, 146–47.

56. *Women's Sharpe Revenge*, p. 109. The superior abstraction of the women's position should be appreciated. From their position as subjects in the relation of domination, they could recognize and attack the *structures* of oppression, and not just the persons of their oppressors.

57. Astell, *Some Reflections upon Marriage*, p. 120.

58. "For the female is, as it were, a mutilated male" (*De Generatione Animalium*, II, 3 [737A25–30]. "Woman is as it were an impotent male because she concocts catamenia (menstrual discharge) and not semen" (ibid., I, 20 [728a18–20]. See *The Works of Aristotle*, ed W. D. Ross (Oxford: Clarendon Press, 1908–1931). See Maryanne Horowitz for a study of these and related passages in Aristotle, including his likening of women to eunuchs, "Aristotle and Woman," *Journal of the History of Biology* 9, no. 2 (Fall 1976): 183–213.

59. *Female Rights Vindicated; or, the Equality of the Sexes Morally and Physically Proved* (London, 1758), pp. 114–20.

60. Mary Astell, *A Serious Proposal to the Ladies, for the Advancement of their True and Greatest Interest*, part 1 (1694; 2d ed. corrected., London, 1695), p. 48.

61. Sophia, *Woman Not Inferior to Man*, p. 20. See also the paraphrase of Sophia, *Female Rights Vindicated*, pp. 47, 51.

62. Astell, *Some Reflections upon Marriage*, p. 76.

63. Marinella, *La Nobiltà della donne*, pp. 47–8.

64. Christine used the lives of the saints as well as Boccaccio's biographies of pagan women. Boccaccio himself drew chiefly from Valerius Maximus, Livy, Hyginus, and Tacitus (Guarino, Introduction to *Concerning Famous Women*, p. xxix). His *De claris mulieribus* initiated a tradition of historical biographies of women—not necessarily feminist—upon which subsequent defenses following Christine's path could and did draw. Vespasiano, the great fifteenth-century biographer, did such a Boccaccio-like work on women, as yet unpublished. In Ferrara in 1497, Fra Jacopo de Bergamo published a collection of the lives of ancient and contemporary women. In England, Thomas Heywood wrote two such histories of women in the 1640s. George Ballard, complaining how women's great-

est achievements were not commemorated, compiled an outstanding collection of the lives of English women from 1400 on in 1752 (now reissued, edited by Ruth Perry). Women also contributed to this genre which, when combined with the feminist perspective that originated in the defenses, may be viewed as the earliest form of women's history. This is certainly the case with Mary Scott's *The Female Advocate* (London, 1774) and Mary Hays's *Female Biography*, 6 vols. (London, 1803). Almost all of these works are still good sources for historians of women. On the biographies of "women worthies" as precursors to women's history, see Natalie Zemon Davis, "Women's History in Transition: The European Case," *Feminist Studies* 3, nos. 3–4 (Spring/Summer 1976): 83–103.

65. Sophia, *Woman's Superior Excellence*, p. 110.

66. Astell, *Some Reflections upon Marriage*, p. 121. Male authors, says the author of *Female Rights Vindicated*, are "prejudiced in their own favour, the virtues and advantages of their sex are everywhere exaggerated; the merit of women is depreciated and debased through an opposite interest" (p. 48).

67. Ibid.

68. For a nice comparison of Boccaccio and Christine, see "Christine de Pizan."

69. Christine de Pisan, *The City of Women*, I.

70. On the tales of the Amazons and the uses they served, see Abby Kleinbaum, *The War against the Amazons* (New York: McGraw Hill, 1983). As this work points out, Christine reconstructed the history of an eight-hundred-year-old Amazon nation in her work on universal history, arguing that this oldest known state proves how well women can govern. See Christine's four-volume *Le Livre de la Mutacion de Fortune*, ed. Susan Solente (1403; Paris: Picard and Co., 1959–66), especially vol. 3, pp. 5–19. See also *The City of Women*, I.19.

71. For Christine's poem of 1429, see *Ditié de Jehanne d'Arc*, ed. A. J. Kennedy and K. Barty (Oxford: Society for the Study of Medieval Languages and Literature, 1977). For Mlle de Gournay's poem, see Schiff, *La Fille d'alliance*, p. 35. Citing her own translation of the Aeneid, she refers to Joan of Arc as "cette illustre Amazone instruicte aux soins de Mars/ . . . Vierge elle ose affronter les plus fameux querriers" (*Egalité des Hommes et des Femmes*, in Schiff, pp. 74, 71).

72. Ester Sowernam, *Ester hath hang'd Haman*, p. 19. For a fascinating linguistic/historical study of the encapsuling of the memory of Boadicea in the ambivalent term dyke, or bull-dyke, see Judy Grahn, "The Queen of Bulldikery," *Chrysalis* 10 (1980): 35–42.

73. On Christine and other early women historians, see Natalie Zemon Davis, "Gender and Genre: Women as Historical Writers," *Beyond Their Sex: Learned Women of the European Past*, pp. 153–82.

74. Ester Sowernam, *Ester hath hang'd Haman*, pp. 19–21.

75. Christine de Pisan, *The City of Women*, I.13.

76. Her book on warfare is called *The Book of Faytes of Arms and Chivalrie* in its English translation; see Bell, "Christine de Pizan," p. 180.

77. On the Italian women, see my "Did Women Have a Renaissance?" chap. 2 above. For the English and French aristocratic women see respectively, Stenton, *The English Woman in History*, pp. 251–52 passim, and Abensour, *Histoire générale*

du féminisme, pp. 147–51. For women as part of European armies, not merely as camp followers and auxiliaries but as combatants, see Barton Hacker, "Women and Military Institutions in Early Modern Europe: A Reconnaissance," *Signs* 6, no. 4 (Summer 1981): 643–71.

78. In Mahl and Koon, *The Female Spectator*. For examples of aristocratic resentment of the exclusion of women "out of all Power and Authority," see Cavendish's address to Cambridge and Oxford demanding equal education for women, and her "Female Orations" in *Philosophical and Physical Opinions* (London, 1655) and *Orations of Divers Sorts* (London, 1662). On Cavendish, see *DNB* 3: 7–9, and Ferguson, *First Feminists*.

79. Marie de Gournay, *Egalité*, pp. 66ff.

80. Epistle, *The Women's Sharpe Revenge*. On Meg, see Patricia Gartenberg, "An Elizabethan Wonder Woman: The Life and Fortunes of Long Meg of Westminster," *Journal of Popular Culture* 17 (Winter 1983): 49–59.

81. The feminists' point, that militant women and women rulers disprove by their very existence the case for woman's "natural" inability to govern, was at once appreciated and blankly denied in the following comment by one of the male scholars of the *querelle*. Referring as they did to Amazons, he thought "feminists seem to have wished to bestow upon women some of the traits to which the more active sex is natural heir" (Utley, *The Crooked Rib*, p. 51).

82. Whereas the religious institutions of Calvinist Geneva worked positively for women, for example, its republican institutions sorely restricted them. See E. William Monter, "Women in Calvinist Geneva, 1550–1800," *Signs* 6, no. 2 (winter 1980): 189–209.

Books on the family and conduct books for women are good sources for these middle-class and classical republican attitudes. Whereas medieval conduct books aimed at making men chivalrous and "noble" for aristocratic ladies, by the late thirteenth century, they began to be directed toward the domestication of girls and women for the approval of bourgeois and also noble men. See Thomas F. Crane, *Italian Social Customs of the Sixteenth Century* (New Haven: Yale University Press, 1920), pp. 358–60. In fifteenth-century Florence, one of the best-known examples of this genre is *Della Famiglia* (1434) by Leon Battista Alberti. Alberti took as his model for his section on domestic economy Xenophon's picture of an Athenian householder, particularly the breaking in of his child-bride to subject her to husband and household. But his departures from Xenophon's *Oeconomicus* are also instructive. Alberti's attitudes are more contemptuous, combining the views of the cleric with those of the early capitalist. He is particularly harsh about erotic love and idleness, both of which he projects onto women and sees as a threat to "manly work." See my reviews in *Italica* 53, no. 2 (1976), and *Renaissance Quarterly* 20, no. 4 (Winter 1967): 483–84. For a fine translation, see *The Albertis of Florence: Leon Battista Alberti's Della Femiglia*, trans. Guido A. Guarino (Lewisburg, Pa.: Bucknell University Press, 1971).

English domestic treatises of this sort, arising from an appeal to the mercantile and craft class, go back to Wyclif, who is believed to have authored the fourteenth-century treatise *Of Weddid Men and Wifis and of Here children*. Once again, the most popular of the English works on women's household duties was Gentian Hervet's translation of Xenophon's *Treatise of Housholde* (London, 1532), which went through six editions by 1573. See Louis B. Wright, *Middle-Class Culture in Elizabethan England* (Ithaca, N.Y.: Cornell University Press, 1935), pp. 201–27. Puritans contributed heavily to this genre in England as it developed in the sixteenth and seventeenth centuries. On the Puritan treatises, see Camden, *The Elizabethan Woman*.

83. Studies are sorely needed on the relation of state formation to the status of women in early modern Europe. Leads may be found in several kinds of works. On women, work, and family, see Natalie Zemon Davis, *Society and Culture in Early Modern France* (Stanford, Ca.: Stanford University Press, 1975); Joan Kelly, "Family Life: A Historical Perspective," *Household and Kin*, reprinted and retitled in this volume, chap. 5; Louise A. Tilly and Joan W. Scott, *Women, Work, and Family* (New York: Holt, Rinehart and Winston, 1978)—all have references to further works. Lawrence Stone's *The Family, Sex, and Marriage in England, 1500–1800* (New York and London: Harper and Row, 1977) surveys many of the political and familial developments for England and has a rich bibliography. On the prosecution for witchcraft of single women living on the fringes of society, see E. William Monter, "Pedestal and Stake: Courtly Love and Witchcraft," in *Becoming Visible: Women in European History*, ed. R. Bridenthal and C. Koonz (Boston: Houghton Mifflin, 1977), pp. 119–36; also, his biographical essay, "The Historiography of European Witchcraft: Progress and Prospects," *Journal of Interdisciplinary History* 2 (1972): 435–51. For economic and social history, Carlo Cipolla, *Before the Industrial Revolution: European Society and Economy, 1000–1700*, 2d ed. (New York: W. W. Norton and Co., 1980), with further references. On law, Sir Frederick Pollock and Frederick W. Maitland, *The History of English Law* (Cambridge: Cambridge University Press, 1898); J. Bellamy, *Crime and Public Order in England in the Later Middle Ages* (London: Routledge and Kegan Paul, 1973); Michael R. Weisser, *Crime and Punishment in Early Modern Europe* (Sussex, England: Harvester Press, 1979).

84. Camden, *The Elizabethan Woman*, p. 254.

85. Spenser, *The Faerie Queen*, V.5, 25.

86. See Allison Heisch's nice demonstration of Elizabeth as "honorary male" in "Queen Elizabeth I and the Persistence of Patriarchy," *Feminist Review* (February 1980): 45–56. For the way the notion of virago was used by Renaissance humanists and its destructive effect upon women of learning, see King, "The Religious Retreat of Isotta Nogarola."

87. Violet A. Wilson, *Society Women of Shakespeare's Time* (New York: E. P. Dutton, 1925), p. 177.

88. Stenton, *The English Woman in History*, p. 142.

89. This episode has yet to be well studied or analyzed for its significance. Reference to it can be found in Wright, *Middle-Class Culture*, pp. 492–93; Camden, *The Elizabethan Woman*, p. 263; Wilson, *Society Women of Shakespeare's Time*, pp. 176–77, 206–8, 211, 214–15, 220–22; and David Harris Willson, *King James VI and I* (New York: Oxford University Press, 1956), p. 304.

Patricia Gartenberg has an interesting note on armed and otherwise "manly" roaring girls of the last two decades of the sixteenth century, named after Thomas Middleton's play, *The Roaring Girl*, (1611). See "Shakespeare's Roaring Girls," *Notes and Queries* 27, no. 2 (April 1980): 174–75. She is concerned with

Long Meg of Westminster and such women who were tavern keepers, laundresses, and so forth. James's concern in the 1620s was with "manly" upper-class women. Chamberlain's reports and the pamphlets cited below indicate this by reference to their liberal allowances, complaints about how women's dress obscures differences in rank, for example. V. A. Wilson and D. H. Willson also see James's campaign as an effort to curb the power ladies of the court had under Elizabeth.

90. John Chamberlain, historian of the court of James I, in *Three Pamphlets of the Jacobean Antifeminist Controversy* (Delmar, N.Y.: Scholars' Facsimiles and Reprints, 1978). See the Introduction by Barbara J. Baines, p. vii.

91. Less than a month later, the historian of James's court reported: "Our pulpits ring continually of the insolence and impudence of women, and to help the matter forward the players have likewise taken them to task, and so too the ballads and the ballad singers . . . and if all this will not serve, the King threatens to fall upon their husbands, parents or friends that have or should have power over them, and make them pay for it" (ibid., p. viii).

92. The author writes of a broad-brimmed hat and "wanton" feather; a French doublet "all unbuttoned to entice, all of one shape to hide deformities, and extreme short waisted to give a most easy way to every luxurious action." These women also exposed "the shame of most ruffianly short locks"; they wore swords in place of needles and strode, not with "modest gestures, but giant-like behaviors" (*Hic Mulier*, in *Three Pamphlets*, A4v).

93. William Prynne, *The Unloveliness of Love-Locks* (1628), quoted by Camden in *The Elizabethan Woman*, p. 226.

94. In Wilson, *Society Women*, p. 4.

95. On this fashion, see Camden, *The Elizabethan Woman*, p. 224.

96. Lillian Faderman describes female transvestism in early modern Europe in *Surpassing the Love of Men* (New York: William Morrow, 1981), pp. 47–62. For some of the symbolic meanings and uses of cross-dressing in early modern Europe, see Natalie Zemon Davis, "Women on Top," *Society and Culture*, 121–51. It should be remembered as part of the history of cross-dressing and the threat it poses that in the 1950s women were arrested in raids on New York City (gay) bars if they did not wear at least two pieces of female attire.

97. Chamberlain, *Hic Mulier*, B2.

98. Chamberlain, *Haec Vir*, B4v.

99. Chamberlain *Mulde Sack*, Bv–B2.

100. Chamberlain, *Hic Mulier*, C2v.

101. On James's ideal of the modest woman and his sumptuary law against the starched yellow ruff worn by both sexes, see Willson, *King James*, pp. 303–4. On Anne Turner, see Edward Francis Rimbault, ed., *The Miscellaneous Works in Prose and Verse of Sir Thomas Overbury* (London: J. R. Smith, 1856), pp. xxxvii, xxxix, liii, ixiii–lxvii; Wilson, *Society Women*, pp. 200–205.

102. On this episode, see Ballard, *Memoirs*, pp. 445–60; Stenton, *The English Woman in History*, pp. 185, 220–28.

103. Women of means also subscribed to books by and on women as another way to subsidize them in eighteenth-century England (Stenton, *The English Woman in History*, p. 241). Ferguson's *First Feminists* will shed some light on

women's networks during the early modern period in England, but much work is needed to uncover supportive connections among feminists. We at least know that Christine, for example, wrote of the groups of women she talked to "as a woman," and Constantia Munda mentioned a group of women with whom she discussed her work. Many of the early feminists knew each other personally; they wrote dedications for each other's books, as Mary Astell did for Lady Mary Wortley Montague; they corresponded, as did Bathsua Makin and Anna Maria van Schurman; and they commemorated each other's learning in their defenses, as Lucrezia Marinella did for Moderata Fonte, and Sophia for Lucrezia Marinella.

104. The *Essay in Defence of the Female Sex* (London, 1696), once ascribed to Mary Astell, has been disputed as hers and is indeed inconsistent with her tone and several of her ideas. Moira Ferguson among others attributes it to Judith Drake.

105. Astell, *Some Reflections upon Marriage*, p. 71.

106. Ibid., pp. 136–37, 146–47.

107. Astell ended the appendix of her book on marriage with a plea to Queen Anne to extend liberty to women, utterly stirred by the vision of what that would initiate: "the women's tracing a new path to honor in which none shall walk but such as scorn to cringe." Queen Anne's leadership could open the way to the millenium when "a tyrannous domination, which nature never meant, shall no longer render useless, if not hurtful, the industry and understanding of half of mankind!" (ibid., pp. 178–80).

108. Knowledge of the number of editions the feminist writings went through and establishment of which authors were incorporated by later ones or were referred to by women readers would be useful. These works were unmistakably written on behalf of women, and in reading them, I felt they were also written *for* women, but we need to discover who their readership actually was as well as the networks of women who supported such projects.

109. Harriet Taylor, "Enfranchisement of Women" (1851), in *Essays on Sex Equality: John Stuart Mill and Harriet Taylor Mill*, ed. Alice S. Rossi (Chicago: University of Chicago Press, 1970), p. 102; Mary Beard, *Woman as Force in History: A Study in Traditions and Realities* (1946; New York: Collier Books, 1962), pp. 287–95; Helen Diner, *Mothers and Amazons: The First Feminine History of Culture* (Garden City, N.Y.: Anchor Press, Doubleday, 1965); Elizabeth Gould Davis, *The First Sex* (Baltimore, Md.: Penguin Books, 1971).

110. Abensour, *Histoire générale du féminisme*, pp. 180ff; Ruth Graham, "Loaves and Liberty: Women in the French Revolution," in Bridenthal and Koonz, *Becoming Visible*, pp. 236–54; Elizabeth Racz, "Women's Rights in the French Revolution," *Science and Society* 16, no. 1 (Spring 1952): 151–74.

FIVE

Family and Society

*T*he title for the following essay was once "Family Life." "Family and Society" more aptly describes its subject: the ways in which people enter the social relationships of kinship, class, and sex through the family; the ways in which these relationships shape the type of family in which we live; and the ways in which ideological norms reinforce them and force us to think they are universal and right.

Unlike other essays in this book, "Family and Society" was written for an audience of advanced secondary and college students and for the general public. It first appeared in *Household and Kin: Families in Flux*, which I coauthored. Florence Howe had suggested such a book as one of a series that was to deal with issues that the women's movement had brought to the forefront: women, work, family, and gender.[1]

Since the beginning of the women's movement, feminists had been concerned with the family as a source of women's oppression. They saw it as an institution in want of redress if the needs of children and parents were to be effectively met. Reactionary political movements were making much of this in or-

"Family and Society" originally appeared under the title "Family Life: A Historical Perspective" in *Household and Kin: Families in Flux*, by Renate Bridenthal, Joan Kelly, Amy Swerdlow, and Phyllis Vine (Old Westbury, N.Y.: Feminist Press, 1980). Reprinted by permission.

der to criticize feminist advances, as if they were responsible for what seemed to be an institutional decay. On the other hand, feminist scholarship in history, theology, and anthropology was turning out surprising information about the durability of family institutions. By the late 1970s, it was apparent that feminists were appreciating a strength and humanity in family life that the earlier movement in the late 1960s would not have believed possible.

My coauthors and I had no set ideas to advance. Rather, we wanted to explore complicated questions that had become even more mystified by ideologies and prescriptions about an "ideal" family life. We divided *Household and Kin* into three parts. The middle, by Renate Bridenthal, was to be on the strains and tensions, the hopes and vulnerabilities, of the contemporary family. The first and third parts were to open up our imaginations about family life and the patterns of domestic arrangements. Mine was the first, an effort to disclose the great variety of families and kin relations in the past. In the last section, Amy Swerdlow and Phyllis Vine dealt with utopian plans for and actual efforts to restructure the family. Our hope was not to advance yet another ideology of what the family should be. Rather, this essay builds on the anthropological, historical, and sociological insights that have come from contemporary feminist scholarship. What it hopes to achieve is liberation from our own prejudices and norms so that we can think through the really problematical issues of our own family and social institutions.[2]

Family and Society

For most of us, the family meets many of our needs for love and support. We tend to think that all families do this in the same way. Yet families are almost as varied as people. Families differ from society to society, and they have changed over time. The anthropologist Claude Lévi-Strauss demonstrated this in a famous essay called "The Family."[3] He noted that anthropologists once thought that "the family, consisting of a more or less durable union, socially approved, of a man, a woman, and their children, is a universal phenomenon, present in each type of society." But, he pointed out, this definition excludes many people. In the case of the Nayar, for example, a people from the

Malabar coast of India, marriages were only symbolic. The warrior life of the men kept them away from home. Their wives were expected to take lovers, and children belonged exclusively to their mother's kin group or matrilineage.

The family arrangements of ancient Sparta were similar to those of the Nayar. The military organization of Spartan society required adult men to live most of their lives in barracks. Their wives lived in households with children whose paternity no one was too strict about, and same-sex love relationships were highly valued. Obviously, the definition of family that the anthropologists started with was too narrow. It was, in fact, a definition of today's nuclear family—which is not universal at all. If we look at the family historically, and in different societies today, we reach the same conclusion Lévi-Strauss did. The only universal element he could find about families was that human beings always form them.

Here we will look at some kinds of families people have established. We will see how people form relations of love and caring, how they have and rear children in families, and how they carry out their society's forms of work by way of families. The patterns of family relations that emerge—of who is considered kin, who lives with and cares for whom, and what is the basic unit for producing and consuming—turn out to be wonderfully varied and frequently changing, even at this very moment.

Kinds of Families

The great variety of family patterns and some of the reasons for it stand out very clearly when we look at societies studied by anthropologists and historians. We will, therefore, first examine families in tribal societies. Then we will turn to family forms that preceded our own, in medieval and modern Europe and the United States. We will see how today's nuclear family emerged out of feudal and preindustrial times. In this historical perspective, we may better understand how the nuclear family developed as it did, why it is undergoing such profound changes, and how the family as we know it might continue to evolve.

Kinship in Tribal Societies. Many tribal societies still exist in parts of Africa, Asia, Oceania, and among the native peoples of the Americas. The question of kin, or who one's relatives are, is more important in tribal society than any other matter. Tribal societies are organized by kin, and life is shaped by the family to which one belongs. Indeed, the question of kin is so elaborate and varied, that it allows one to see how even the relation between children and parents is socially, rather than biologically, formed.

Paternal authority over children as we define it is the authority of a biological father over his children. This form of authority is nonexistent in many places. Among the Nayar, for example, it is the mother's brother who is economically responsible for, and has authority over, his sister's children. The biological father has only a ritual relation to his offspring.

This denial of paternal power goes so far among the Trobriand Islanders and the Wunambal of northwestern Australia, that it is an official belief of both societies that men play no role in the biological conception of children. Such beliefs need not be due to ignorance. They are probably another way of asserting that the maternal uncle is the only socially recognized male parent.

Children in certain parts of Tibet and Nepal have a different kind of male parent. Men are seminomadic here. They work as guides and bearers of goods and are off in the mountains for long parts of the year. Several men, usually brothers, marry the same woman, who keeps a common household for them. This marital arrangement of one woman with several husbands is called polyandry. All the children regard as "father" the husband who officially becomes father of the household by a special family ceremony. In this case, we speak of a social father. Fatherhood is recognized, but it is not a biological matter. It is socially agreed upon, and the position may be transferred to another of the husbands by means of the same ceremony.

Another example of how the relation of father is socially rather than biologically formed is in a family where children have one woman as mother and another woman as father. Among several peoples of Africa, such as the Fou of Dahomey and the Lovedu of South Africa, women of high rank marry "wives" who bear children to them by unacknowledged lovers.[4] The noble woman is regarded as the "father" of the children. In accordance with the father's right in those societies, she passes on to "her" children, whom the wives bear, her name, status, and wealth.

In none of these cases does biological paternity lead to fatherhood in the sense of special emotional ties, economic responsibility, and authority over children. The biological father is not a parent to his children in ways that we would recognize.

Motherhood tends to be a more stable matter. The biological mother is usually the socially recognized mother, too. However, females other than the mother often take on maternal responsibilities. Child rearing tends to be a community activity in the more egalitarian, tight knit communities of tribal society. Even nursing is shared. Children nursed by several women often regard these women as their "other mothers." These may be their mother's sisters, as in south and central Australia. Or, in polygamous societies such as the Tupi-Kawahib of central Brazil, the several wives of a chief act as mother to all the children.

Collective mothering also occurs in societies where children are raised in matrilineal houses. This arrangement is common among horticultural people who live by cultivating plants and raising some animals for food. The longhouses of the Iroquois of North America held twenty-five or so mother/children units, in villages of about 2,000 people. The houses and the children raised in them belonged to the mother's line of descent. A husband moved into the house of his wife—and moved out again if the conjugal unit of wife and husband dissolved, which it frequently did. Among the Iroquois, the matrilineal household was a far stronger family unit than that of mother, father, and children.[5]

The Atjehnese of Sumatra have a similar pattern of matrilineal kin and households.[6] In place of longhouses, they live in separate huts that cluster in compounds. The huts and compounds belong to sisters and mothers' sisters. Ownership of the houses and often of the rice land the women cultivate passes through the maternal line to daughters. The Atjehnese women control the group's basic means of subsistence, much as the Iroquois matrons were in charge of the distribution of food and other stores. Hence, women in both cases enjoy the authority that goes with economic power.

In societies organized by kinship, then, as most tribal societies are, children's relation to their father and mother may vary. They may be subject mainly to maternal authority; to matrilineal authority exercised by the mother's brother, as well as by the mother and her sisters; or to paternal authority exercised by a ritually chosen father—who may at times be a woman. The children's household may be a collective one in which the girls may remain but the boy will have to leave. Or, in yet another variation, children may be reared in an individual household by their biological mother and father, both of whom are socially recognized as their parents.

Growing Up in Feudal Society. Feudal societies existed in early Greece from the fifteenth to the twelfth century B.C., in Japan from the twelfth to the sixteenth century A.D., and in medieval Europe from the late fifth to the fourteenth century.[7] Although economic and political life was organized by alliances among kin groups, in feudal society a small minority of such groups, who possessed military power, controlled almost all the landed property and wealth. This warrior aristocracy exercised sovereign power—of war and peace, life and death, and taxation—over the populations that worked the land for them. This contrasts with the more communal tribal societies where there were (and are) no great distinctions in wealth and power. In political terms, feudalism is thus seen as intermediate between tribal, kinship society and class-based society organized by a state (called a *polis* by the Greeks, giving us our word *political*). In its family patterns, too, feudal society was both distinctive and intermediate. Its organization by kin groups gave certain families and the women in them powers they would lose as states developed. The sharp class divisions of feudal society, however, kept military and economic power in the hands of a very few families.

In the case of medieval Europe, family life differed greatly depending on whether one belonged to the warrior aristocracy or the laboring serf class. It also took different forms for those who entered the Church. These three social groups were called "the estates" in feudal Europe. The clergy was the first estate. The warrior aristocracy was the second, and the laboring class, mostly serfs, made up the third estate. Children were reared very differently to fit them for these very different stations in life.

Children of the ruling aristocracy were trained to advance the powers and class positions of their kin, or family line—chiefly by arms, but also by marriage and by means of high position in the Church. The aristocracy ruled over its counties, duchies, towns, and territories by a complicated system of exchange. Great lords (or, sometimes, ladies) gave lands "in fief" to vassals. The vassal, who was always a warrior, or male member of the aristocracy, governed the fief, which might consist of one or many units of manorial land. Income from the fief supported the vassal and his warrior dependents, but the vassal never owned the lands he held from his lord. Vassals had to give military service and other dues in return for a fief, and this bond between vassal and lord could always be renewed, or broken.

Sometimes, vassalage coincided with kin ties, but often it did not. The warrior class was itself divided into ranks that ranged from mere knights to powerful counts, dukes, barons, and members of royal families. Within the aristocracy, individuals advanced themselves and their family line by allying with more powerful, higher-ranking families. Vassalage and marriage were two ways these kin groups made political alliances with each other.

To serve the needs of their family line, children of the aristocracy were sent away from their parental households when they were very young. At about eight or ten years of age, but sometimes even earlier, they joined a household of superior rank. This might be the "court" or residence of their father's lord, of a powerful maternal uncle, or of a ducal or a royal family. Education at court consisted in part of training in arms, for warfare. The tournaments and jousting of the Middle Ages were displays of this kind of skill. Girls often became skilled at weapons and riding, too, because they could, and often did, take over fiefs to preserve the family property in the absence of male heirs, or when their husbands went off to war. Because noblewomen could serve their kin and husbands as managers and/or heirs of fiefs, they had genuine power in medieval society—particularly in the higher ranks of the aristocracy. This gave them a commanding position in the second major area of courtly education: training in courtesy, or chivalry. Children, and all those residing at court, were expected to develop manners befitting their noble way of life, and it was largely ladies at court who shaped these courteous manners.

Courtesy included courtly love, which has had a great influence on modern notions of romance. In medieval society, however, this love relationship was not connected with marriage. Young knights were encouraged to devote themselves to the love of a lady at court, who might often be the lady of their lord. This is the case in the most famous romances of the time, such as that of Lancelot and Guinevere or of Tristan and Isolde.[8] In these stories, adultery is clearly idealized as a form of love. Yet courtly love actually supported the institutions of the feudal warrior aristocracy. From his service to his lady, the lover was supposed to learn how to be faithful and self-sacrificing—the primary virtues of any vassal. Moreover, men were away a great deal of the time in this warrior society, and marriages were political alliances, not emotional ones. The courtly romances probably reflect an acceptance of extramarital love that responded to these situations and to the fact that children were assets in feudal society, as potential warriors and wives. If children should be born out of wedlock, they were usually adopted formally or informally as members of their biological father's family line, or they were accepted in their mother's household as children of her and her husband's line.

The development of courtly love was opposed by the Church in medieval and early modern Europe, although not too successfully.[9] Because the Church held that its nuns and monks, and all members of the clergy, should be celibate or nonsexual, it did not reproduce itself biologically. Its ranks had to be filled from the aristocracy and peasantry. The Church claimed that celibacy was a spiritually superior state. This seemed to entitle its members to superior social status. Indeed, the Church, which was one of the greatest landowners of medieval Europe, sought to rule over the kings and emperors of the feudal aristocracy, as well as over serfs. The religious life officially excluded sexuality. This kept the Church's wealth from falling into the hands of heirs. The sexual views of the Church also kept women out of the clergy. Although women could be nuns and could rule over convents and convent lands as abbesses, women could not be priests, bishops, or popes.

The Church sought to limit sex for the laity to heterosexual union, and to make that union a lifelong, monogamous marriage. It permitted sexuality only for procreation. In this sense, the Church tended to strengthen family ties among wife, husband, and children. It opposed extramarital love, as well as the aristocracy's frequent use of divorce to gain new lands and allies by way of new marriages. At the same time, for children moving into adulthood, the Church offered an alternative to marriage and family. The Church or convent became a substitute family for those who entered it. Noble families sent daughters and younger sons who would not inherit land into the Church, where they assumed powerful positions as bishops, abbots, and abbesses. Those children of serfs who served the Church moved into more lowly positions. They became priests on manors, or humble nuns and monks.

Like children sent away to court, many children destined for the Church began their training quite young. In convents and cathedral schools, upper-class children, and some from the lower ranks, learned Latin—which was the language of the Church, and also the only written prose language until the thirteenth century. When universities developed in the course of the twelfth century, they were open only to those who had this basic Latin training. University students were educated for high positions in the Church hierarchy, and for positions within the universities themselves. They were all clerics or clergy. As clerics, university students were all men. Education in civil law was the only area of learning open from the first to lay people. Even though in later centuries, higher education was opened to lay people, certain clerical attitudes have clung to academic life. With very few exceptions, women were excluded from higher education down to the late nineteenth century, and only in the twentieth century have fellowships come to be held by students who are not unmarried men. Even today, medieval caps and gowns are worn at graduations.

Neither training at court, nor at church schools, was open to the large majority of young people in feudal society, male or female. While the Church prayed for the "soul" of feudal Christian society, and the aristocracy "protected" or controlled it by force of its arms, the third estate or social group, mostly serfs and some few artisans and merchants, fed that society. The labor of the third estate supported the Church and the aristocracy. The serfs tilled the lands of medieval Europe, and for their children there was no education except in the tasks that enabled them to replace their parents.

The status of the serfs was midway between slavery and personal freedom. They were bound, not to individual owners, but to the manors on which they were born. Every serf family had its own cottage and its own lands to till. But, in addition, serfs paid a variety of rents and taxes in the form of labor, as well as in animals and food. They had to pay a tithe, or tenth part of their income, to the Church and do heavy labor for the manor besides. They worked the lord's land as well as their own. They kept the walls of the lord's castle in repair, built the roads, and carted wine and supplies to their lord's lord. They paid their lord each time they used the manor's mill to grind their grain. They paid for the oven to bake their bread, the press to make their wine. And it was the lord's manorial court that tried and fined—or executed—them.

Because for centuries there was more land than there were peasants to cultivate it, marriage outside the manor was forbidden. This ensured that children would take over the labor of their parents. Thus, serf children were raised in their family cottage and worked alongside their parents from early childhood. Their life was confined to the manor, its village, and the local church. And with life defined by the daily and seasonal round of work on the land, they had little time for play or self-cultivation, except for Sundays and holy days.[10]

The Preindustrial Household. In Europe in the fifteen and sixteenth centuries, feudalism was replaced by state-organized societies, although vestiges of the feudal system remained for centuries. With this shift came changes in the nature of the family. The household with its resources—usually land—became the basic unit of economic production. In place of the common lands of a tribal village, or the medieval manor which supported several serf families as well as its lord, private property emerged. That is, the individual household-family owned its own means of subsistence.[11]

In this preindustrial household, the position of men, and especially of the father, was greatly strengthened. The father owned the household and its resources. Usually he passed it on to his sons—either to the eldest, by primogeniture, or to as many as he wished. During this period, laws were enacted that favored inheritance in the male line. State laws also supported paternal authority in the household. Hence sex, as well as kin and class, shaped in new ways the experience of family members.

Because of the power vested in the father in the preindustrial household, this type of family is called patriarchal (from *pater*, the Roman word for father). The patriarchal family contrasts with the matrilineage of the Iroquois and Atjehnese, for example, and with the family organization of medieval Europe too. Although feudal society recognized paternal authority, an aristocratic wife's kin protected her interests, and everyone treated children more as members of the family line than as property of their fathers. Women and children of medieval serf families belonged as much to their lord (who might be a lady) as to their husbands and fathers. Widows and daughters in both classes could inherit the positions of men as long as they carried out the services that went with them. And in both serf and aristocratic families, fathers did not own their family property (which really belonged to the manor or to their lord), so they could not dispose of it at will.

As state-organized societies developed, the privately owned property that most often sustained the work of the patriarchal household was land. Some households also supported themselves through craft production. Many farming families in England, for example, worked the land but also spun and wove cloth at home which they sold to merchants. Merchants, artisans, and shopkeepers in the sixteenth, seventeenth, and eighteenth centuries combined home and workplace in a similar way, although their property was not in land. This small group was called the bourgeoisie in Europe, from the towns or *bourgs* (Cherbourg, Edinburgh, Strassbourg) in which their way of life developed. Or they were called "middle class," because they were midway between the serfs who were not free and the aristocracy who were free but did not labor. They were free, but they had to work for a living. Typically, these members of the bourgeoisie worked with property that their families owned.

Their households usually consisted of a shop or store, with living space in the rear or on the upper floor. The father generally owned the household and passed it on to one or more of his sons. Most of the members of the family, along with apprentices, lived in the household and worked at the craft or business together.

The poor of sixteenth-, seventeenth-, and eighteenth-century Europe and America also supported themselves within the patriarchal household. Since the poor had little or no property of their own, they worked and often lived in someone else's household. They were often bound to their work, or indentured, but unlike medieval serfs and American slaves, their period of service was limited. Poor children left their parents at an early age to begin their service in another's household. From seven years on, they labored for masters who provided work, room, and board—and discipline as well. They worked as farmhands, apprentices, and, if they were girls, as domestic servants. Apprentices in the crafts were usually indentured at fourteen for a period of seven years. At the end of their period of service, these young people hoped to have training in some skill or craft, or to have acquired some land and small items of furnishings with which to form a household of their own.

Heads of households—usually fathers of its core nuclear family—had the same authority over indentured youths and live-in laborers as they had over their own children and relatives. Everyone who dwelt and worked within a household obeyed the father as if he were parent to them all. In 1715, Daniel Defoe described that paternal power this way: "Masters of families are parents, that is guardians and governors, to their whole house, though they are fathers only to their children." [12] Hence, fathers were often called "the Governor." English farm wives referred to their husbands as "Master" well into the nineteenth century, [13] and even older parents or single brothers supported by a father's household bowed to his authority.

As masters, fathers could be tyrants, and many were brutal. Whipping, flogging, and child beating were common in the preindustrial patriarchal household. The propertied classes of the time believed in "breaking the will" even of their own children.

It is from them we learn that "to spare the rod spoils the child," and they certainly did not spare the foster children and live-in servants who worked for them.

Not all people could be, or wanted to be, supported and governed in this paternal way. But state laws and need for work pressured them to do so. In seventeenth-century New England, where the settlers could easily regulate their small populations, it is claimed that virtually everyone who was not a household head or his kin was the servant or apprentice of one. It is in New England, too, that the relation of household work to marriage and sexual activity is clearest. Apprentices, lodgers, and domestic servants were expected—like children—to live with their masters until they had acquired the means to marry and form households of their own. Until that time, the master was supposed to guard their chastity, for Puritan New England in particular frowned upon sexual activity outside of marriage.[14]

Paternal control of sexuality is common wherever we find the patriarchal household/family. The father controls the marriages and sexual lives, as well as the work lives, of all members of the household in ways that best support its economy. It is to his interest, and the interest of the household economy, that young men marry late. Sons under this system often delay marriage until their late twenties or thirties, until the father parcels out some of his land to them, or passes the homestead on. Live-in laborers must wait until they have earned enough to buy land or other means of subsistence to start their own households. In the meantime, the young men give the patriarch the labor he needs.

Girls and women are just as strictly controlled in this kind of family. They have no hope of heading a household, as long as the pattern of inheritance favors their brothers and sons, as it did in Europe and the United States. In the sixteenth, seventeenth, and eighteenth centuries, propertied families therefore sent their daughters to households more prosperous than their own, to do some kind of service. They might be companions—really personal maids—to the woman of the household. Or they might be governesses. Poorer girls were placed quite young in other people's households to do spinning or domestic work.

Young women often found their future husbands among associates in the households they went to. Their marriages were arranged either by their own father or by the master. Girls or women who did not find husbands could look forward only to continued domestic or other work, in their parental or other households. Marriage seemed preferable, because it put a woman in charge of the domestic arrangements of her husband's household. She might be called the mistress of the household, although it was "his" household, and wives were expected to give obedient service. Peasant wives all over Europe did not sit at the table when the husband and boys ate; they served them.

In all these situations, the sexual life of girls and women was supervised by heads of households who were usually male. This sometimes led to abuse, particularly if the household was very powerful or isolated. Then the local community could not act as a restraint the way the small medieval village or town could. In other cases, paternal authority led to strict sexual suppression. Unlike the aristocratic feudal family, there was no room in the preindustrial household for children born outside of marriage. The preindustrial family's resources were more limited; and whatever the sum of household property, it had to be divided among "legitimate" male heirs.

For the vast majority of Europeans and Americans in the sixteenth, seventeenth, and eighteenth centuries, the household and its resources formed the pattern of work and family life. As the basic economic unit for most people, it tended to make the family synonymous with whoever lived and worked within the household, rather than with groups of kin.

The preindustrial household, however, did not form the pattern of family life either for the most privileged or for the most oppressed. The aristocratic families of Europe did not live unto themselves in a household, or support themselves by its means. Aristocrats often lived at royal and princely courts. They continued to send their children to court and convents for their early training, and moved their young men into high-ranking positions in the Church, the military, and the government. Until the French Revolution and even later, until they ceased to be a legal ruling class, the aristocracy considered their kin group or lineage to be their family. And they maintained the class status of their lineage by marrying only into other aristocratic families. Ever since the age of courtly love, their sexual practices had been quite free. This was due in part to their privileged position in society, but also to the fact that marriage for them served chiefly the class interests of the family line. It had little to do with household economy, or even with bonds of affection and sexuality. Indeed, marriage was often ruled out altogether for younger daughters and sons of the aristocracy so as to keep the landed estates of the family line intact.

At the other end of the social scale, the slaves of the southern United States had neither the property nor the personal freedom that formed the basis of the preindustrial household. They were themselves property of the landed proprietors they worked for. And they lived in shacks on the master's land, unlike indentured servants who lived in the household of a master for their limited term of service. The Afro-American slaves raised their children in two-parent families when they could, however.[15] Their domestic ties were close-knit, even though these ties were often cruelly severed by forcible sale. Teenage children were most likely to be sold out of the family, but marriages between young parents could also be broken. From letters that have been preserved, we get some sense of how frequent and painful these separations were. One family could not be reunited after emancipation, for example, because the husband had married again after he was sold to a new owner. "I would come and see you," he wrote to his first wife,

> but I know you could not bear it. I want to see you and I don't want to see you. I love you just as well as I did the last day I saw you, and it will not do for you and I to meet. I am married, and my wife have two children, and if you and I meets it would make a very dissatisfied family.
> Send me some of the children's hair in a separate paper with their names on the paper. Will you please git married as long as I am married. My dear, you know the Lord knows both of our hearts. You know it never was our wishes to be separated. . . .[16]

Black slave families also formed strong kin networks. By naming children after fathers, aunts, grandparents, and other blood kin in both the maternal and paternal lines, they kept track of family members forcibly separated by sale. Kin networks also provided the comfort of family connections to slaves sold into another locality. The web of strong domestic and kin ties formed by Afro-Americans made possible their emotional and, later, their economic survival in a hostile surrounding community.

Class, or social status, may thus account for departures from what the rest of a society takes to be the family norm. In other instances, changes in the norm come about as a society at large begins to adjust to new social developments. Population changes, such as changes in sex ratio due to war or to a prohibition of infanticide, may affect traditional patterns of marriage and work. Polygamy tends to occur when there are more women than men, for example. And the polyandrous situation of one wife to several brothers that was common in parts of Tibet and Nepal grew up in a context of girl infanticide.

Changes in family form also come about with changes in patterns of work. These may be due to the loss or gain of property such as slaves, land, or mineral wealth, or to new ways of organizing work and property. When Europe and the United States industrialized, in the nineteenth and twentieth centuries, work and property were reorganized so drastically that we still call this process the industrial "revolution." It was then that the nuclear family developed—but not in the same way for all classes.

The Nuclear Family

Today's nuclear family descends from the preindustrial household/family. Industrialization was the main reason for the change in the family pattern of the household. With industrialization, goods and services came to be produced outside the household. The household ceased to be a center of production— although it remained as an economic and residential unit for its members.

First cloth and clothing, then all manner of goods, including the machinery for producing them, came to be made in factories rather than shops and homes. In factories, groups of workers were gathered in one place and organized to work together. Together, they produced large quantities of goods that had previously been produced by an individual or a small group of household workers. This is called social production, and it soon replaced privately organized household work.

The property that supported this new social production of goods changed, too. Instead of land and the handlooms and spinning machines of the farming household, instead of the simple tools and skills of the artisan, came the kind of property called capital. Industrial capital includes money, plant (factories and machinery), and raw materials. Large sums of money were needed to purchase machinery and raw materials like cotton, coal, and iron. Money paid for the labor that transformed raw materials into products that could be sold. And ever larger sums of money from the sale of those products were reinvested in new plants and more materials.

Separating Work and Home. England in the late eighteenth century, then western Europe and the United States, were the first to undergo this shift to social production. In increasing numbers, people went to work in factories and mines. They laid the railroads that formed a network for the exchange of materials and goods. And as they went to the new mill and mining towns and to the cities, they were forced to leave the land behind them. Farming and household production could no longer support them as it had for centuries. Society became urbanized with industrialization. In 1870, out of every 100 people ten years or older in the United States, there were 48 men and women who worked the land. In 1970, there were 3 farm workers out of every 100 people sixteen years or older in the United States.[17]

Agricultural products were still needed, of course. In fact, urban life stimulated farming and the raising of livestock, as city dwellers needed food. Large-scale agricultural businesses developed to meet the mass demand, particularly in the United States. That is, farming, too, became capitalized. By using expensive machinery, large agricultural businesses could produce more food than small household farms. They also required far fewer workers. Throughout the nineteenth and twentieth centuries, as farmers found they could not compete with the big agricultural businesses, they sold or abandoned their small family farms. This drove even more people to the cities to look for work.

Capital in the form of large sums of money, machinery, and materials thus came to provide the means of work for most people. The social organization of work, whether on the land or in factories, mines, and transportation industries, replaced much of the work once done in private households. And as cities developed, small family businesses—just like small family farms—gave way to larger, more powerful operations. Banks and stock companies, insurance and law firms, large department stores and food chains, financed, insured, and sold the new products of industrial society. Large numbers of white-collar workers were needed to sustain these growing businesses, and so in the early decades of the twentieth century, masses of people became clerks, stenographers, telephone operators, salespersons, brokers, and lawyers. Their work, too, was socially organized.

In all forms of this socially organized work, people work outside the home. Wages are their means of support—in place of private family property in the form of land or small shops. Thus, the patriarchal preindustrial household lost its productive function. We are still experiencing the consequences of this major change in family life.

The most immediate consequence was that the household became merely a home. That is, it ceased to be a center of production, although it remained the center of family life. As the household lost its land or shop, most of its members also moved out by day (or night) to work for the wages that now bought their food and paid their rent. However, home was the place that supplied the sustenance, comforts, and necessities wage earners required to get to work the next day. Thus, some work remained in the home. The work of transforming the income and goods that came from outside into the necessities and pleasures of daily life—meals, clothing, decent living quarters—remained in the home. Such work was necessary to sustain the family and raise the next generation, and it was mostly women with children who stayed at home to do it.

The notion of who makes up a family changed, too. The family shrank in size as it gradually lost the apprentices, live-in laborers, and kin who had dwelt within the household when it was a place of employment. In predindustrial times, the members of a household were regarded as a family. As industrialization proceeded, only the nucleus of the patriarchal household/ family remained at home. Gradually, the nuclear family of parents and children became the new family norm.

The Division of Family Labor. When work was separated from the home, the family ceased to work together as a unit. This divided the sexes and the generations from each other in new ways. Women and children worked in factories during the early stages of industrialization. After that, however, it was mostly men who had the jobs in factories, mines, and businesses. Woman's place was said to be in the home. Since children were also based in the home, they, too, were cut off from the work life of adult males. Socially organized production seemed to separate women from men, and children from their fathers, keeping women and children in the private domain of the home.

Historically, the exclusion of women and children from the world of social labor and public life occurred first in modern times in the wealthy bourgeois families of Europe. The feudal aristocracies knew no such division. Their court and manor houses were the centers of social and public life. Nor did most working people know any division between family and work. Labor was parceled out by sex and age in the serf family and in the later preindustrial household—but the workplace was not divided. This was as true of artisans and small shopkeepers as it was of peasants and farmers. Work and home were bound together, and so were the daily work lives of women and men, children and adults. But among the wealthy bourgeoisie in Europe, and by the nineteenth century in America, the divided pattern of the nuclear family emerged.

Originally, the owners of capital were called the upper middle class (or haute bourgeoisie in French). They were not considered the upper class as the aristocracy held that position. In the preindustrial period, this upper segment of the bourgeoisie invested in commerce, mining, and textile production, as well as in land. In the late eighteenth and nineteenth centuries, with industrialization, they put the wealth they had made in trade, banking, and other enterprises into the new factories, mines, and transportation systems. All these sites of capital investment were outside the home. The upper middle class defined this entire sphere of work as man's world. They extended this notion to the state, too. Politics was for them a male domain, just as it was a class domain from which workers and farmers were excluded.

This capitalist class became the dominant group, economically and politically, in nineteenth-century Europe and America. It became the real upper class, replacing the aristocracy of the past. As in the old aristocratic upper class, women in these capitalist families became "ladies," when their fathers, brothers, and husbands became wealthy and powerful. Doing no work outside the home, and with servants inside it, they were leisured like aristocratic women of the preindustrial period. Like them, they enjoyed a class privilege. But bourgeois women were more restricted than aristocratic women had been. They were considered domestic creatures at a time when men's activities were all outside the home. Their lives were more segregated from men's than aristocratic women's lives had been. The new ladies of the capitalist class and wives of the middling professional groups (lawyers, doctors, churchmen, and professors) who served them were told they had no role in the public world. Women's lives were confined to the private sphere and defined by the domestic functions of "consumption" and "reproduction."

The affluence of men was demonstrated by the cost of supporting women. By "conspicuous consumption," a newly arrived capitalist family gave notice to society that it was making its way into the ranks of the rich. The idleness of women, the servants they required to maintain them, their cumbersome dress and delicacy, were part of the display of bourgeois wealth and power. Even in the lower and middling middle classes, men gauged their status by whether or not they could afford to keep their wives and daughters at home. At home, bourgeois women were less idle than they seemed. They had a heavy burden of entertaining to aid their husbands' business and professional careers. Though hostessing—with its dinner parties, elaborate exchange of invitations and thank you's, and fine cuisine—falls under the category of consumption rather than production, for women it was work. It was work, too, to cater to the emotional needs of one's husband. And the most valued work of bourgeois women was in the sphere of reproduction—bearing and rearing children.

Indeed, motherhood was the *only* function society came to recognize for "ladies"—until women themselves forced a change.[18] The women's movement of the second half of the nineteenth and the early twentieth century was largely a struggle of upper-middle- and middle-class women to break out of the limits imposed by marriage and the mothering role. They demanded education and professional training, the right to work and be active outside the home, and control of their own income and property. At the same time, because the mothering role was so esteemed, many affluent women adopted it, but extended it to society at large. This was especially true in England and the United States. Florence Nightingale was one of many gifted women who worked tirelessly, often without pay or official position, to supply housing, schools, and health care to nineteenth-century children, workers, and soldiers. Women did volunteer work to meet the social needs that industrial capitalism created, but which business and political leaders ignored.

The energies of most upper-middle- and middle-class women in the nineteenth and early twentieth centuries were confined to the nuclear family, however.[19] Marriage was their means of support, and motherhood made them the vessel through which family ownership of property passed from generation to generation—in the male line. Bourgeois women did not inherit or control economically significant property. And in the late nineteenth century, they were just beginning to overcome educational barriers and laws that kept them out of business, the professions, and politics. Their rights of divorce were limited. They often had no claim to their children, and if they did separate from their husbands, they had little possibility of supporting themselves.

The economic dependency of women upon men could be a burden to bourgeois men, too. It bound men as well as women to marriage and made them solely responsible for the material well-being of their families. Yet marriage and family served men in many ways. Men had the economic rewards and public recognition of achievement in the world, as well as the comforts and rewards of home and family. A family—especially sons who would inherit their gains—gave them a reason for spending their lives on business. And at the end of days spent in a hard-headed competition, they could return to the home as a refuge.

Wives provided emotional support, tender sentiments, and a compliant relationship. A wife was supposed to be "the angel of the hearth," and children were to be seen but not heard.

Children also became economic dependents in the bourgeois home. Unlike children of working-class families, children of the rich, and even children of the growing middle class, did not have to go to work. Their leisure brought advantages and disadvantages. A childhood and adolescence without work made possible greater cultural development. On the other hand, it postponed adulthood. Economic dependency kept youths of the wealthier classes subject to the authority of their families, and that authority continued along patriarchal lines. Fathers kept their daughters at home well into the early twentieth century, while their sons went to boarding school and the university. But for both girls and boys, the bourgeois father was a forbidding, authoritative figure. He was distant, yet completely in command.

The distance of the bourgeois father was emotional as well as physical. Business outside the home kept him away from his children and absorbed his interests. Moreover, loving, supportive attitudes were supposed to be womanly, as well as unbusinesslike. At the same time, this often harsh, barely known person continued to control all the property of "his" family. This gave him a concern for, and power over, both the sexual lives and the careers of his children.

Girls were reared to marry a suitable member of the propertied class. Their social lives were closely watched and they were brought up in extreme modesty. The more "protected" and sexually ignorant they were, the more apt they would be to obey the will of their fathers. Even though the upper middle class widely accepted the double standard, according to which women had to adhere to a stricter moral code than men, fathers also controlled their sons' sexual lives. Daughters and wives were guarded because they were to bear the heirs to family wealth. Sons had to concentrate on making that wealth. Any sign of sexual interest or activity was suppressed in their youth. Sexuality and love had to take second place to economic interests, and the marriages of young men, like those of their sisters, had to serve the family's ambitions.

In this kind of family life, sexuality was not supposed to be visible. It was veiled with Victorian prudery—as the rebellious generation of the 1920s would call it. Live-in servants, who were chiefly women, were expected to be celibate. To be a "maid" meant to be an unmarried maiden, as well as a servant. Pregnancy was hidden. Certain topics and words could not be mentioned in polite company. At dinner, one asked for "white meat" rather than breast of chicken. Even the legs of pianos were covered in a "proper" home. All this modesty kept sexuality and pleasure in the background, repressed in the interest of productive goals.

In this atmosphere, tensions naturally arose around sexuality and the power of the husband and father. They were suppressed in the family, but they found an outlet in art and science by the end of the nineteenth century. Plays such as Henrik Ibsen's *A Doll's House* exposed women's resentment about their passive, doll-like lives. Sigmund Freud developed psychoanalysis, a therapy to release repressed emotions. His upper-middle-class patients, he found, were suffering in adult life from the sexual feelings they had not been allowed to express in early childhood. Today Freud himself is criticized for some of his patriarchal notions. Yet his work contributed to a powerful critique of the patriarchal family life of his time. Repressed feelings of love may be necessary to sustain family authority, but they lead to symptoms of mental distress that Freud called neurosis.

Working-class families also became nuclear with industrialization, but there is a great difference between them and families of the bourgeoisie. Everyone in a working-class family had to work.[20] In the early 1900s, only a third of foreign-born families in the United States could live on the wages of a male "head." Most young children worked on the land or did odd jobs in the towns. They ran errands, peddled things, tended store, took care of still younger children, and helped their mothers doing piecework at home. At ten and twelve (and routinely at as young as five in nineteenth-century England and the United States), they went into mines, factories, and sweatshops.

These girls and boys were part of the wage-earning labor force. They worked as hard and as long as adult men. But in the mines and mills, the highest-paying jobs were reserved for the men. Children and women never earned enough to live on.

They were used as unskilled workers, had the lowest rates of pay, and often worked the longest hours. They also worked in unhealthy and unsafe conditions. Young children labored long hours underground in the mines. Others spent all the daylight hours in mills, and accidents were frequent because workers were not protected from dangerous machinery. The labor laws that were meant to protect young children and women from such abuses came late, and only after a great deal of struggle. In 1908, the minimum age for child labor in the United States was set at ten years, and health and safety standards for children began to be imposed. Gradually, compulsory schooling also reduced child labor. Protective legislation was extended to women workers, too, but there were no laws to secure equal work or pay for women until the 1960s and 1970s.

Because wages were so low among industrial workers, family life was a means of survival as well as a source of affection and human warmth in lives brutalized by poverty. Only by pooling their wages could working-class people hope to feed and house themselves. Youths and immigrants who came to the cities alone usually moved in with other families, as in the days of the preindustrial household. Now, however, they went out to work and paid for their room and board with money rather than labor. Since wages gave them freedom to move, they were less subject to patriarchal tyranny than apprentices and servants had been in the preindustrial household.

Thus girls and boys, young women and men, went to work outside the home. In this major sense, the working-class family differed from that of the owning class. Yet there was a similarity between the two groups in the family's division of labor. In both kinds of families, most mothers remained based in the home.

Working-class mothers often needed to earn wages as their husbands' pay was usually low. Sometimes their husbands were sick, disabled, or unemployed. Some mothers became widows or were abandoned. But working-class mothers were handicapped in earning a living. The care of children claimed their time. And if they returned to waged work, they had to suffer the low pay and long hours allotted to women and still care for their families when they got home. Employers, unions, the fact that society made individual mothers solely responsible for children, all kept married women out of the labor force. As late as 1920, 90 percent of the female labor force in the United States was made up of single women.[21] How many of them merely claimed to be single we do not know. Nor do we know how many were forced to remain single so as to support parents and other family members.

Keeping married women out of factories, offices, and even schools did not keep them from working for pay, however. It simply bound them to unskilled, underpaid, and unpaid work in the home and outside it. Married women took in boarders and did piecework at home for textile factories and laundries. They did other people's sewing, laundry, and housework. And aside from whatever "productive" work they did for pay, the primary job of working-class mothers was unpaid child care and housework.

Like the ladies of the bourgeoisie, the working-class mother took care of her family's reproductive and consuming needs. That is, she did the necessary cleaning, shopping, cooking, child care, and nurturing to maintain her family. Attending to those tasks in the home without servants was a full-time job. And increasingly, as the twentieth century progressed, the homes of the middle class, like the homes of the working class, were without servants. Most women did most of the work of maintaining their families themselves.

Women's Work in the Home. In the industrialized United States, until as late as the 1970s, the majority of married women worked exclusively in their own homes. Despite changes in technology and different levels of family income, most twentieth-century mothers have spent their days doing housework and caring for the children and whatever other relatives live in the home.

Housework is a catchall term that covers a number of tasks done at home. Obtaining food is one aspect of housework. For some families, food raising is still a part of household work. Historically, the more men did socially organized wage work, the more women and children became responsible for the farming, gardening, raising of chickens, and so forth that supplied some of the family's food. This happens when the family still owns or rents some land. As urban life grew at the expense of rural life, however, food was bought rather than raised. Then shopping became a basic part of housekeeping.

Cleaning, preparing, cooking, and serving food in the form of meals call for different skills. Contemporary housewives report that next to child rearing, they like cooking most among their various tasks. It is creative and is usually appreciated. Cleaning up after meals, cleaning the home so that it is orderly and usable, keeping the furnishings and clothing of the family in good condition (and in an earlier time, making cloth and clothing), make up yet another complex of jobs. As skills, laundering, ironing, and mending bear little relation to each other, or to housecleaning, and many housewives say they are not particularly satisfying tasks. They are monotonous, because they are constantly repeated and never completed. And they are generally not appreciated. This work is noticed only when it is not done—when a shirt is missing a button, a bed not made, a floor not clean.

Add child care to housework, and we begin to see why the job of "housewife," according to a study done in the 1970s, takes an average of seventy-seven hours a week.[22] Most housewives who have been surveyed say that child rearing is the most rewarding part of their work. They also speak of the conflicts it sets up with the other demands of housework and of life in general. The care of children has little in common with housekeeping—except that in nuclear family arrangements, both are carried out in the private home, usually by the same person: the mother. Child care requires a set of skills and interests that are sometimes directly opposed to those required by housekeeping—and by husband care. Should one keep the floors clean or let the children play? Does one follow the rhythms of young life or force children into the schedule of a working father?

Moreover, not every woman has the attitudes and interests child care calls for, or can sustain an interest in children all day long, day after day. Infants need and have a right to close attention, feeding, fondling, changing, and stimulation for play and learning. Young children also need and deserve loving attention to their bodily, emotional, and imaginative needs. Some mothers are fully satisfied with their daily work in the home. Others have conflicting feelings. They enjoy their children, but feel the loneliness that child care in the isolated home imposes. They sometimes speak of the despair that overtakes them as they face the daily routine of endless caring for others with no time for their own needs. The resentment and guilt that build up often create unhappiness.

Over a hundred years ago, an English feminist pointed out that there was no good reason to expect that every mother enjoyed, or was even particularly good at, meeting children's daily needs. It was also wasteful, Harriet Taylor Mill wrote, to require each and every married woman to stay in her home all day with her children. Women who really enjoyed children could set up a nursery for several such families. This would free the energies of those who might have other talents and interests.

Harriet Taylor also noticed that child rearing in the private home by the mother was coercive. That is, mothers had no choice in the matter, because there were no other socially acceptable arrangements. On the one hand, society said it was "natural" for married women to stay at home and care for children. And on the other hand, society refused to employ married women, or even educate them so as to fit them for other jobs. If full-time mothering was so natural, she queried, why did it have to be enforced this way? Why were the prejudices and even laws against educating women, and about employing mothers, if they "naturally" took to staying at home with children?

Of course, there is nothing natural about any way of raising children, or those ways would not be so varied. Social custom, not nature, determines what mothering means. Well into the eighteenth century, for example, the aristocratic upper classes of Europe sent their infants to wetnurses until they were weaned at three or four. Urban women who worked as silk spinners and artisans did the same.[23] The wetnurse was usually a peasant who had just recently given birth herself and had a nursing baby of her own. She took in one, and sometimes more, babies and nursed them—as women in the preindustrial household did—while carrying out her work and life in the countryside. Ironically, even among the nineteenth-century bourgeoisie—the group from which we inherit the idea that women are chiefly mothers—the reality was quite different from the ideology. Affluent women of this period frequently handed over the care of their children to servants or slaves—the nannies, governesses, and black mammies who did the daily work of mothering.

Men's participation in child care also varies in different cultures and different eras. In tribal societies, a network of female and male kin often care for each others' children. They are all "daughters" and "sons," looked after by the entire group. Among the Arapesh of New Guinea, Margaret Mead observed that the father as well as the mother is said to "bear a child." The father as well as the mother stays with the infant and meets its momentary needs. Both father and mother are held responsible for child care by the entire community. Indeed, she goes on to say, "if one comments upon a middle-aged man as good-looking, the people answer: 'Good-looking? Ye-e-s? But you should have seen him before he bore all those children'"[24]

What? Men give birth? That may be a little too remote from our experience, although several societies have such notions. What is familiar from our preindustrial period, however, is that fathers were closely involved in the daily work of raising children. The father's role in the preindustrial household included teaching and disciplining. He particularly trained the boys of the household in their future work skills. When fathers left the home to work in factories and offices, the sexual division of labor with regard to child rearing was sharpened. Compulsory schooling took over many of the father's tasks. This brought the benefit of literacy to children, but it meant that fathers lost control over training the boys of the family. It also meant that care of younger children fell almost entirely to women, especially to mothers, who were becoming ever more isolated as everyone else left the home each day for school or for wage work.

Nursing makes up a final set of tasks that has been assigned to women in the home. Until the development in the twentieth century of hospitals and nursing homes as places of treatment and care, even great ladies were supposed to care for the ill of their household, including servants and slaves. As with child care, however, servant women did the most difficult physical tasks of nursing. Today people get much of their medical and nursing care outside the home. But such care is expensive. It is not available to everyone. Thousands of rural communities in the United States lack even one doctor, and they do not have systems of transportation to any medical care. Even in cities, health care is often unavailable or too costly for most low-income families. When this is the case, nursing still falls to the wife and mother. Indeed, it is often regarded as one of her duties even when a family can afford professional care. Families expect to be nursed by mother, even though today's mother does not have the help of relatives in the home, any more than she has servants.

Combine nursing—which also includes attending to the emotional needs of all family members—with the demands of child care and the chores of housework, and we can see why "a woman's work is never done." What is harder to understand, is why people also say that housewives "don't work."

The tasks performed by the housewife are necessary, time-consuming work. One of the main reasons housework is so time-consuming is that it remained private while other work was socially organized. Studies conducted in three countries show that, despite household appliances, the hours spent on housework have not decreased from 1929 to the 1970s.[25] The housewife does not get paid for these hours of work. She does not charge for the meals, housecleaning, laundered clothing, and nursing she provides, any more than she charges for child care. And because she is not paid, her work does not get economic recognition. This sometimes makes it seem as though she doesn't work at all. Yet, clearly, she does work that *can* be paid for.[26] For pay, a housekeeper or a team of housecleaners can do the family's housekeeping—and they do, in certain income groups. With higher family income, restaurants or a hired cook can provide meals. Laundries, dry cleaners, and tailors can take care of furnishings and clothes. Although these paid services may not be ideal substitutes for the unpaid work of housewives, they enable us to measure the real costs of housework.

The reason housewives have not been paid is because they are the last group in industrial society to do their work in their homes. No member of the preindustrial household was paid for labor. The household simply housed, fed, and clothed them. Only apprentices and live-in workers earned some small pay, and even they worked mostly for room, board, and training. No one worked just for wages until labor was socially organized outside the home. But then, only those who went out to work got that wage.

Through the late nineteenth century and into the twentieth century, working men in factory after factory organized to demand a "family wage." This wage was meant to support *all* the necessary work of the family. It was to take the place of the property once owned by the individual household. Since working families could no longer own the property now needed for their work—the mines, the factories, the machines—since they could no longer raise their own food, or sell the products of their labor, the family wage supplied the means of subsistence for a family unit. The family wage was distributed very unevenly, however. Only organized workers in certain skilled occupations received it, and they, by definition, were adult males.

Women had to continue in the pattern we have described—whether they were the few supported by the family wage of a husband, or the many who were not. Single, they could not earn enough to live independently. And married, they could not hold on to decent, full-time jobs outside the home. A married woman had little choice but to do all the work that remained to be done in the home. That work enabled her husband and the older children to go to their jobs every morning. But since they got the wage that supported her labors in the home, it seemed to pay for their work only. Thus, housewives were—and are—said to do their seventy-seven hours a week labor just "for love."

If women who worked in their homes were paid, even at one dollar an hour, we would begin to appreciate their labor. We would notice that housewives work—and for longer hours, less pay, and none of the benefits of the male wage earner. The conditions of work in the home would become clear, along with the attitudes women, men, and children have toward it—and each other. As of now, the housewife is always on call to serve the family's "needs" for comfort, service, and care. On the one hand, it is her job, so no one is expected to perform these services for her. On the other hand, it is no job at all—so along with no pay, she gets no days off, no vacation, and no retirement. Today, even married women employed outside the home do about forty hours a week of housework. That is ten times more than married men do, in the care of what is also *their* home and children.[27]

This, then, is how the nuclear family emerged from the pre-industrial household. Socially organized production changed the quality of family life, as well as of work. With most kinds of work done outside the home, families came to depend on wages, rather than their own property, for the necessities of life. And as capital squeezed out household property, the household master lost his position, too. He was no longer master of his economic fate. He was still master in the home, however. Only the bourgeois husband and father continued to own property that supported his wife and children at home and at school. Yet working-class people also experienced the division of labor that marked the new, bourgeois economic order. In the work force, adult men—although often impoverished, exploited, and unemployed themselves—nonetheless earned wages consistently higher than youths and women. And in the family, although mothers and children also worked, they were dependent upon the wage of an adult male as their main means of subsistence. The family thus continued as a patriarchal, economic unit.

Although families no longer work together in a household, they still form households—residences in which the income and labor of all the members are pooled. As families, they carry out the tasks necessary for social life. Their work in home, factory, and office has been reorganized by industrial, capitalist society; but families still work to sustain themselves and raise the next generation.

It was out of these historical developments—the introduction of wage work and the division of family labor—that our image of the ideal family arose. Daddy leaves the home to go to work. Mommy stays home cooking and cleaning. And there are Dick and Jane at school, learning skills and attitudes that will fit them for the work their mother and father do. Yet we know that this is not a true picture of all family life—not in the past, and certainly not now. Today, something is happening to the nuclear family which is exciting and disturbing. It is affecting us all.

Family and Sex Roles in Flux

A striking change is taking place in the United States in patterns of family life. Over the last twenty years, the "traditional" nuclear family has become less and less typical. Today, the nuclear family with father working outside the home and mother and children at home "not working" can hardly be regarded as the norm.

As we have seen, this "ideal" nuclear family was never quite what it seemed to be. Even in families of higher-paid skilled workers and professionals, who came closest to living according to the nuclear family ideal, women's work in the home helped support the family. Women and children were dependent on the father's wage, however. This obscured the fact that father and children were also dependent on mother's work in the home. And it made schooling seem like a gift, rather than a new form of training for work in industrial society. In many other families, the discrepancy between the real and the ideal was even more striking. Where fathers earned less money, children held jobs after school and ended their schooling early to be able to work full-time. Married women, especially in new immigrant groups and among racial minorities, earned money, if only at low-paying, part-time jobs. And, of course, some adults lived alone, some lived with children in single-parent families, and some lived as unmarried couples.

Today, however, only 7 to 15 percent of American families fit into the nuclear family norm of father at work and mother at home with the children.[28] Two major developments account for this fact. One is the dramatic increase of married women in the work force. The other is equally dramatic but less evident—the growing number of adults who live in households without children. These changes in work and population patterns are closely related, and both lead to a new sense of the relations between children and parents, women and men, families and society.

Mother Has a Paying Job. Women now make up about half the labor force in the United States. And where married women were only 10 percent of the female labor force in 1920, that figure rose in 1976 to 75 percent. The great increase in women workers has been among married women, particularly among mothers.[29]

Half of all mothers of school-age children are wage earners in the United States today.[30] The reason has to do in part with the continued organization of work outside the home. The same development of socially organized production that made men wage earners is now making wage earners out of women, mothers included. On the one hand, the steadily rising costs of clothing, food, housing, schooling, nursing, and health care that can no longer be provided by the household make mothers seek paying jobs. And on the other hand, jobs open up as the goods and services that women once provided in the home come to be commercially made and sold. Now, as ever, women generally work because they cannot afford not to. But now, even when they are married, they—like men—work full-time for wages outside the home.

The entry of married women into the labor force has had profound effects upon family and sexual arrangements. These effects are being felt by almost everyone. They are not just private matters. Nor are they temporary. Married women are apparently in the labor force to stay.[31] They need to be there if their families are to survive. Yet married women cannot work outside the home without other changes taking place. Who cares for children—and who cares for adults? These become urgent questions, and they call for social as well as personal responses.

The care of children is a major social concern as well as a family one. Children are essential if a society is to survive. Yet our society has not found ways to provide loving, educational surroundings for millions of children whose parents are working outside the home. By 1976, 37 percent of mothers who had children under six were employed. At the same time, only 1.7 percent of the 16 million children of wage-earning mothers found places in child-care centers.[32] Where were all the other children? Some were cared for at home by other relatives or by paid child-care workers. Some were cared for in other people's homes. And some were home without any care at all. The quality of such care in the home (or lack of it) is very varied.

Families that most need the mother's income are the ones least able to pay for the nurseries and centers that are available. Publicly supported child-care centers are rare. Government, which is in charge of public funds, has not assumed this responsibility in the United States as it has in other countries, such as Sweden. Nor has industry, which employs workers and sets their rates of pay. There seems to be a great reluctance on the part of these powerful social institutions to meet the physical, emotional, and intellectual needs of the next generation.

Moreover, some parents object to child rearing outside the home. Others, however, argue for the benefits of rearing small groups of children together, under the guidance of supportive adults. They also see child care outside the home as an opportunity to have men as well as women care for young children. But those who oppose nursery and day-care centers fear that children cared for by others will not feel they "belong" to their families. They fear depersonalized, noncaring situations— which can in fact come about when lack of funds and support make nurseries mere baby-sitting centers.

Since mothers are working outside the home because they must, however—and ever more will be doing so—someone has to take care of children. Perhaps fears about nurseries and day care can be met by demanding *good* child-care arrangements. Working families clearly need nurseries and child-care centers. Public and/or employer-funded centers should be made available. Yet families could still oversee the kind of care their children receive. These centers could be made as accountable to parents as the costly private ones are.

As more married women enter the labor force, relations between the sexes also change. These changes are causing controversy, too. In part the problems that arise have to do with work. When both parents work outside the home, there is a need—on women's part, at least—for a fairer sharing of what remains of housekeeping and child care in the home. It is not simply unjust for one of the parties who works all day to shop, prepare dinner, clean up, care for the home, and care for the children. It is physically draining and emotionally abusive, too.

Sharing family work may seem fair and logical and be threatening nonetheless. Girls and boys have been brought up expecting women to be economically dependent on men. The norm was for men to bring in the income. Women were expected to be inept at business and politics, poor at figures—but emotionally supportive of husbands and children. They lacked authority, but they were supposed to be "naturally" good at the domestic work that served their family's needs.

The family's division of labor has been the greatest shaper of sex roles. Generations of children have learned to relate to each other in terms of mommy and daddy's pattern of behavior—or what it was *supposed* to have been. They learned to become feminine and masculine, according to the nuclear family norm. Women were "feminine" if and only if they did women's work in the home. Males who did such work were ridiculed. School and work reinforced the family's division of labor and paternal authority as well. Sports, mathematics, engineering, law, and business were male pursuits. Reading, nursing, teaching elementary school, and clerical work were for women. The labor force reflects this pattern even today. Women are employed at low-paying, sex-segregated jobs. They earn only 60 percent of what men earn. And women almost always report to male bosses.

Today, women make up about half the nation's paid workforce. Will society continue to cling to the idea of "woman's place" and resist what we might well call mothers' rights? Most women still become mothers. Since almost half the mothers of the United States work for pay, they are surely right to demand access to all kinds of jobs, and wages equal to men's. In 1980, their pay is low, their working conditions poor, and their job status inferior. As long as we insist that the old norm still holds, and that mother's place is in the home, the *real* situation of mothers suffers. Indeed, the situation of all women—and of the families they work to support—suffers. Employers rely on the old nuclear family ideal to keep women's wages low. Since "normally" women are supported by men, employers argue, why should they expect a fair wage?

Children, men, even women may cooperate in this myth—for fear of what equality between women and men might mean. If women are full agents in society, their role as perpetual motherers will have to change. But does this mean that women and men will form a sharing relation in the family, whereby they both serve each other and their children? Everyone is afraid of losing something familiar in gaining this new equality—even if the familiar now conflicts with family needs. Both children and men can gain a great deal if fathers participate fully in child rearing. With women earning money, men lose the burden of sole responsibility for the income of the family. But men also lose the service and patriarchal authority that went with their economic power. Women may have ambivalent feelings about shared parenting. On the one hand, they do not want always to be the only person children turn to; on the other hand, that role offers some satisfactions. And by gaining equality, women also lose the right that minors have, to be dependent.

Divorce, which now ends one of every three marriages (and one of every two first marriages), may reflect these new pressures in part. Many women who resent an unfair division of family work and authority are now economically able to change their status. Divorce does not seem to threaten the family as an institution, since most divorces lead to remarriage. The high divorce rate seems rather to point to a need many people feel to restructure their marital relations.

Equal work and responsibility in the family means that girls and boys, men and women, will have to learn to relate to each other differently outside the home, too. They will no longer be boss and helper. They will be teammates, co-workers, and voices of equal authority. Such change in status and power affect everything—from who makes the beds and changes the diapers to who governs the country and sits in judgment in the high courts of the land.

A Longer and More Varied Life. There are other important reasons, in addition to mothers working outside the home, for changes in family life. Changes in family size, life expectancy, marriage, contraception, and divorce also make families depart from the old norm. And they, too, give rise to needs and practices that are new and controversial.

The move toward smaller family size in a way defines the nuclear family. As the household ceased to be a center of production in the nineteenth and twentieth centuries, the family, in the sense of who lives in the home, had to become smaller. Those who once found work in the household and on its land had to leave it to find wage work. Only the nuclear core of the preindustrial household remained—consisting of parents and children. This change in the composition of the household occurred gradually. At first, workers lodged with families near their place of work and paid for room and board. Around 1900, in urban centers such as New York City, only 50 percent of the households of working people were made up of just the nuclear core.[33] But the "exodus of adults" from the family, as it has been called, continued. Fewer and fewer homes continued to hold a widowed grandparent, a maiden aunt, unmarried adult children, or an unrelated lodger. These are people who live alone today. From just 1940 to 1970, there was a 12 percent decline in family size—and three-quarters of that decline was due to the shrinking number of adults in the family.[34] Young adults leave home earlier, before they are married. Older ones continue to live alone after the death of a spouse.

Along with this kind of reduction in family size, families are also having fewer children. This development is a further reason for making us question why mothers should be confined to the home. It contradicts the nineteenth-century definition of woman's role as lifelong mother. Mothers now have fewer children, and have them more closely spaced, than ever in history. Families need, for their 1.8 children per family, only two to four years of infant care.

The declining birthrate is connected with changes in mortality (death rate). So is the increase in divorce. The frequent death of children and adults down to the middle of the nineteenth century made for family patterns very different from our own. Marriages, for example, lasted from twelve to seventeen years for the preindustrial peasantry of Europe. People entered their first marriages later than we do. They had to wait until they had enough property to start a household. Many people without property did not marry at all. Women who did marry, were twenty-four or twenty-five years old in eighteenth-century England and France. Men were about twenty-seven. Such couples seldom lived long enough to raise their children to adulthood. After about fifteen years of marriage, one of the parents would die, usually the mother in childbirth. That first marriage would be followed by a second, and the raising of a second family.

This meant that most children lost at least one parent as they were growing up. Many of them would be raised in households with stepparents, half-brothers and sisters, and perhaps with some orphaned cousins, too. Preindustrial society was more youthful than our own. Mortality was very high among infants and children, so more children had to be born to replenish the adult world. In seventeenth-century England, for example, one-quarter to one-third of all the children born died before they were fifteen. In one well-to-do family, the wife, who had married at nineteen, bore twenty-one children before her husband died. Yet only four daughters and one son survived her.[35]

Today most people marry young. Wage-earning couples do not have to wait until they inherit the family land or shop, or save up a dowry. At the same time, life expectancy has almost doubled. The death rate in Europe and the United States is down to about one-third of what it was in the eighteenth century.[36] Changes such as these explain why families are now choosing how long to stay married, and how many children to raise. Death no longer decides these matters for us.

Today's pattern of divorce and remarriage actually recreates the marriage pattern of preindustrial families. It seems to be less disruptive to the family life of children, however, than the old pattern of death and remarriage. The percentage of children under fourteen who lose a parent by death or divorce has been decreasing. In the United States, that number fell from 27.8 percent in 1900 to 19.1 percent in 1978. The total percentage of children who live in families with at least one of their natural parents is also increasing.[37] Wage work does away with the preindustrial practice of fostering, sending out children to other households. And it now permits women to raise children on their own if they need or want to.

The declining birthrate, like divorce, is another response to changes in life expectancy. Modern nutrition, sanitation, and medicine have dramatically reduced the death rate among infants and children. This is less true for the poor in the United States and throughout the world, where malnutrition and lack of health care still claim the lives of many children. In general, however, most children who are born in industrialized countries now live to adulthood. And now that death does not limit the number of children families can raise, families tend to limit the number of births.

The reduction of births has been made easier, yet more controversial, by the technology of mass contraception. Almost all societies have sought to limit (or increase) their numbers in relation to their resources. Some of their methods seem inhumane to us. Eskimos let aged parents perish, for example. In ancient Greece, Arabia, and in Nepal until very recently, female infanticide was widely practiced. Today's contraceptive technology can resolve some of the problems other societies have faced, but it raises many problems of its own. Women's groups and health groups are very critical of the dangerous side effects of the most widely used female contraceptives. Some religious denominations oppose abortion, and some oppose all forms of contraception. Other groups representing poor women and racial minorities argue that lack of public funds for family planning coerces such women to accept sterilization. Sterilization, which is publicly funded, is irreversible, whereas contraception and abortion permit continued choice.[38]

Here as elsewhere in matters concerning the family, there is conflict, controversy, and change. While most people who have been surveyed support the right of women themselves to choose if and when they will bear a child,[39] other groups and many laws still oppose this. At the same time, there are new reasons for limiting birth today. In addition to changed mortality rates and the cost of raising children in an advanced industrial society, there is the question of the relation of the world's people to its resources. Some argue that births should be drastically reduced where resources are scarce. Others point out, however, that food and other necessities simply need to be fairly distributed. Actually, it is now economically possible for all children who are born to live and thrive. It is economically possible for all to have the food, health care, housing, and education they need. The potential is there for a humane and socially just control of birth and death—if social policy is geared to a fair distribution of resources and to the rights of women to bear as well as not to bear.

Whatever one's moral position on birth control, the fact of its spreading use is socially important. Changes in patterns of life and death, modern modes of work, awareness of the need to distribute the world's resources fairly—all account for today's smaller families, as does the will of women and families to exercise choice in having children and in spacing births. The desire to limit births, and the ability to do so, in turn affects our notions about sexuality. Indeed, much of the opposition to contraception and abortion has to do with this. There is fear that birth control will disrupt the bond between sexuality, marriage, and family.

It is important, in dealing with this issue, to notice that the declining birthrate affects how many children will be raised in a family, *not* how many people will be parents. If anything, more people get married today, and become parents, than ever before. Preindustrial society kept entire groups of people unmarried— sons and daughters with no inheritance; apprentices, servants, and journeymen; spinners (spinsters) in textile centers; soldiers, prostitutes, monks, nuns, and priests. Yet sexuality was more tightly bound to family and marriage than it need be today. It is possible today for women and men to lead lives together without raising children. It is economically possible, and birth control makes it biologically possible, too. Since this does not threaten the social order as it did when society was founded upon the patriarchal household, the childless family and the unmarried couple living together have become more acceptable. The same is true for lesbian or male homosexual couples. Women also are now more able to raise children in single-parent families or in collective households.

Such changes in sexual patterns and living arrangements are social facts today. They are part of the context within which we make our moral choices. Even though society is particularly slow in accepting departures from the norm in regard to sexuality, options are now opening for those who have no wish to live in nuclear family arrangements. Neither marriage, parenting, nor raising children in a family is on the decline. But those who wish to live otherwise are able to move a little more openly into alternative family situations.

One final, but major, alternative pattern has yet to be mentioned. It ultimately affects most people, and it is one of the chief reasons why only 7 to 15 percent of today's families fit the old norm. What has been called the most radical change in the twentieth-century American family is how long parents now live alone after their children leave home. Couples who now marry at twenty and twenty-one tend to have few children, to have them soon after marriage, and to space them closely. That means they are in their early forties when their children start living on their own. This is a family situation almost all of us will face. Yet it is one our society has barely begun to reckon with. It is a new pattern—parents living out long lives of their own without children, and continuing to live on, often alone, after the death of a spouse.

Almost half the people who live alone today are over sixty-five. They are retired, often against their wishes. That means they are isolated from social networks that work generally provides, and they live on reduced incomes. Families, who could once give social and economic support to their elders, no longer have the resources to do so. Wage-earning families do not have space to house aging parents, relatives, or friends. They do not have family members at home to attend them. Nor do most families any longer need the abilities and skills of older people. Many middle-aged people will feel anguish and guilt toward the older generation, in the belief that families somehow should provide the space, time, and attention their elders deserve— when, in fact, they cannot. As with child care, new social arrangements are called for. Ties of affection between the generations are probably as strong as ever, but traditional modes of family care have broken down—and new modes have yet to emerge.

Like children in today's society, older people are victims of the most recent changes in the nuclear family. It is as though the present, ever more nucleated form of family life serves only those who work, or are being trained to do so. The family, for them, is a residential unit. It is the primary unit for consumption and reproduction. It is the unit within which we find affection and support. But the numbers of people we can extend that family support to are shrinking. Our very young and our old need some new connective tissue to bind them to society and give them vital support. They, and perhaps all of us, are in need of some sustaining social associations—age-integrated sport and cultural centers, local health and nursing centers, neighborhood gardening groups, block associations, self-help groups—networks to mediate between the wage-earning family and the work-oriented society it is now so dependent upon.

Loss of the old nuclear family norm does not mean the end of the family, or even of the nuclear family. It does mean that our development as a society has carried us beyond what we once viewed as normal, or ideal, patterns of family life. Some of those patterns were more myths than realities, as we saw. The major flaw in the notion of the ideal nuclear family was that it made children and women appear idle, as if they no longer took part in the necessary work of society as they had in the days of the preindustrial household. Actually, all that had changed were the modes of work. Adult male labor outside the home was recognized and waged. The schooling of children that replaced apprenticeship was not. Nor was the work of women in the home. Since neither children nor women received wages, it seemed as though they did not work. Yet without their labor, the work force could not be sustained or replaced.

Steadily, however, married women and mothers were drawn into the paid work force, too. It is increasingly necessary now for mothers to work outside the home to support themselves and their families. But because child rearing in the private home has not been viewed as socially necessary work, no social provisions have been made for care of preschool children or for older children after school hours. This is one of the urgent, unresolved problems of our time.

Women and men are also experiencing strains because of the sex roles assigned to them in terms of the old nuclear family ideal. As women gain economic independence, they seek to take on their share of family work. It is clear that men lose some of their old patriarchal prerogatives as they lose sole control of the family's resources. On the other hand, there are new possibilities for democratic family relations and for shared responsibilties. The course our society will take here is not yet certain.

Other developments that carry family life beyond the old norm have to do with changes in family size, life expectancy, marriage, and divorce. The frequency of divorce, and the fact that there are fewer children in today's families, sometimes make it seem as though the family is disappearing as an institution. Yet these signs of fragile family life prove deceptive, as we saw, when placed in historical perspective. More children than ever in recent history are now reared within their families by at least one of their natural parents. What has changed here is simply that lower mortality rates for infants, children, and adults now make possible choices about family size and duration of marriage that people did not have before.

Making such choices raises conflicts with traditional values, however. Divorce and contraception are far from universally accepted, for example, even though they are becoming more widespread. There is also controversy over, and a growing acceptance of, alternate family arrangements. All these developments emerge from new patterns of work and population changes, but they raise problems nonetheless. It is a little like the potential we now have for longer, more varied lives—a potential that confronts us, at the same time, with a need for new social forms if we are to realize it in creative, fulfilling ways.

Every generation has to find its own way of shaping its institutions. But perhaps having surveyed the past—having seen the great variety of family forms humans have devised, and the reasons for the evolution of our own—we may have a surer sense of the social possibilities and problems before us.

Notes

1. The other authors were Renate Bridenthal, Amy Swerdlow, and Phyllis Vine. The Feminist Press published the series and the book. Amy Swerdlow was our chief editor, Liz Phillips of the press our in-house editor. *Household and Kin* is indebted to them both.

2. The ideas in this essay build on a decade of feminist theorizing about the family. Using perspectives that are historical, cross-cultural, social, and psychoanalytic, these writings have helped to broaden our understanding of the changing and varied relationship of family structures to the condition of women in society. Especially important are Nancy Chodorow, *The Reproduction of Mothering: Psychoanalysis and the Sociology of Gender* (Berkeley: University of California Press, 1978); Chodorow, "Mothering, Male Dominance, and Capitalism," in *Capitalist Patriarchy and the Case for Socialist Feminism*, ed. Zillah R. Eisenstein (New York: Monthly Review Press, 1979), pp. 83–106; Zillah Eisenstein, "Some Notes on the Relations of Capitalist Patriarchy," in ibid., pp. 41–55; Heidi Hartmann, "Capitalism, Patriarchy, and Job Segregation by Sex," in ibid., pp. 206–47; Rayna Rapp,

"Family and Class in Contemporary America," *Science and Society* 42 (Fall 1978): 278–300; Rayna Rapp, Ellen Ross, and Renate Bridenthal, "Examining Family History," *Feminist Studies* 5 (Spring 1979): 174–200; Adrienne Rich, *Of Woman Born: Motherhood as Experience and Institution* (New York: W. W. Norton, 1976); Gayle Rubin, "The Traffic in Women," in *Toward an Anthropology of Women*, ed. Rayna Reiter (New York: Monthly Review Press, 1975), pp. 157–210; Mary Ryan, *Womanhood in America from Colonial Times to the Present* (New York: Franklin Watts, 1975); Louise Tilly and Joan Scott, *Women, Work, and Family* (New York: Holt, Rinehart and Winston, 1978); and Eli Zaretsky, *Capitalism, the Family, and Personal Life* (New York: Harper Colophon, 1976).

3. Claude Lévi-Strauss, "The Family," in H. Shapiro, ed., *Man, Culture, and Society* (London: Oxford University Press, 1971). His large study of tribal society is *The Elementary Structures of Kinship* (Boston: Beacon Press, 1969). For a critical evaluation, see Eleanor B. Leacock, "Structuralism and Dialectics," *Reviews in Anthropology* 5, 1 (Winter 1978): 117–28.

There are several useful studies of domestic arrangements in band and tribal societies in two anthropological collections: Rayna Rapp Reiter, ed., *Toward an Anthropology of Women* (New York: Monthly Review Press, 1975), and Michelle Rosaldo and Louise Lamphere, eds., *Woman, Culture, and Society* (Stanford, Calif.: Stanford University Press, 1974).

For the history of childhood, the classic study is Philippe Ariès, *Centuries of Childhood: A Social History of Family Life* (New York: Vintage Books, 1962). See also, Lloyd de Mause, ed., *The History of Childhood* (New York: Harper & Row, 1975), and John R. Gillis, *Youth and History* (New York: Academic Press, 1974).

For younger readers see Barbara Kaye Greenleaf, *Children Through the Ages: A History of Childhood* (New York: Barnes & Noble Books, 1979).

For lucid definitions and analysis of "family," "kin," and "household," see Rayna Rapp, "Family and Class Contemporary America," *Science and Society* XLII, 3 (Fall 1978): 278–300.

4. On the Lovedu, see Karen Sacks, "Engels Revisited," in Reiter, ed. *Toward an Anthropology of Women*, p. 225. On the Fou, see Melville Herskovits, *Dahomey* (Evanston, Ill.: Northwestern University Press, 1967), pp. 320–22. For other instances of female husbands and male wives, see Denise O'Brien, "Female Husbands in Southern Bantu Societies," in Alice Schlegel, ed., *Sexual Stratification: A Cross-Cultural View* (New York: Columbia University Press, 1977), and Gayle Rubin, "The Traffic in Women," in Reiter, ed., *Toward an Anthropology of Women*, p. 181.

5. Eleanor Leacock, "Women in Egalitarian Societies," in Renate Bridenthal and Claudia Koonz, eds., *Becoming Visible: Women in European History* (Boston: Houghton Mifflin, 1977), pp. 11–35.

6. Nancy Tanner, "Matrifocality in Indonesia and Africa and among Black Americans," in Rosaldo and Lamphere, eds., *Woman, Culture, and Society*, pp. 129–56.

7. The classic study of European feudal society is Marc Bloch, *Feudal Society* (Chicago: University of Chicago Press, 1964), 2 vols. Also useful are Sidney Painter, *French Chivalry* (Baltimore: Johns Hopkins Press, 1940), and Eileen Power, *Medieval Women* (Cambridge: Cambridge University Press, 1975).

8. For medieval romances, see *Arthurian Romances*, trans. and ed. by W. W. Comfort (London and New York: Dutton and Dutton Everyman's Library, 1970) and *Lays of Marie de France* (London and New York: Dent and Dutton, 1911). Poems by women troubadours are in *The Women Troubadours*, trans. and ed. by Meg Bogin (New York: Paddington Press, 1976).

On courtly love, see Joan Kelly-Gadol, "Did Women Have a Renaissance?" chap. 2; Emily Jane Putnam, *The Lady* (Chicago: University of Chicago Press, 1970), chap. 4; and Maurice Valency, *In Praise of Love* (New York: Macmillan, 1961).

9. On the Church and universities, good introductions are Marshall W. Baldwin, *The Mediaeval Church* (Ithaca, N.Y.: Cornell University Press, 1953); Geoffrey Barraclough, *The Medieval Papacy* (New York: Harcourt Brace, 1968); and Helen Waddell, *The Wandering Scholars* (London: Constable, 1932).

10. On serfdom, see G. G. Coulton, *Medieval Village, Manor, and Monastery* (New York: Harper & Row, 1960). Medieval history and its institutional development are best presented by Henri Pirenne, *A History of Europe* (New York: Anchor Books, 1958), 2 vols.

11. A basic, very readable work on the preindustrial family is Louise Tilly and Joan Scott, *Women, Work, and Family* (New York: Holt, Rinehart & Winston, 1978). For reference, see Lawrence Stone, *The Family, Sex and Marriage in England, 1500–1800* (New York: Harper & Row, 1977).

12. Stone, *The Family, Sex and Marriage* p. 156.

13. Doris Mary Stenton, *The English Woman in History* (New York: Schocken Books, 1977), p. 117; Stone, *The Family, Sex and Marriage*, p. 199.

14. For a good collection of articles on the family in Europe and the United States, see Michael Gordon, ed., *The American Family in Perspective* (New York: St. Martin's Press, 1973). See especially the essays by John Demos and Edmund Morgan on New England.

15. On the black family, see Andrew Billingsley and Amy Tate Billingsley, *Black Families in White America* (Englewood Cliffs, N.J.: Prentice-Hall, 1968); John W. Blassingame, *The Slave Community* (New York: Oxford University Press, 1972); Herbert G. Gutman, *The Black Family in Slavery and Freedom, 1750–1925* (New York: Random House, 1977); and Carol B. Stack, *All Our Kin* (New York: Harper & Row, 1974).

16. Gutman, *The Black Family*, p. 6.

17. Jim Watts and Allen F. Davis, *Generations: Your Family in Modern American History* (New York: Alfred A. Knopf, 1978), p. 201.

18. On bourgeois women and the women's movement, see Barbara Corrado Pope, "Angels in the Devil's Workshop: Leisured and Charitable Women in Nineteenth Century England and France," in Bridenthal and Koonz, eds., *Becoming Visible*, pp. 296–324, and Edith Hurwitz, "The International Sisterhood," in *Becoming Visible*, pp. 325–45.

19. On the bourgeois family, see Eli Zaretsky, *Capitalism, the Family, and Personal Life* (New York: Harper & Row, 1976).

20. On nineteenth- and twentieth-century working children and wives, see the later chapters of Tilly and Scott, *Women, Work, and Family*; also Mary Lynn McDougall, "Working-Class Women during the Industrial Revolution, 1780–

1914," in Bridenthal and Koonz, eds., *Becoming Visible*, pp. 255–79, and Theresa M. McBride, "The Long Road Home: Women's Work and Industrialization," in *Becoming Visible*, pp. 255–80.

For the United States, see Rosalyn Baxandall, Linda Gordon, and Susan Reverby, eds., *America's Working Women* (New York: Random House, 1976), and Mary Ryan, *Womanhood in America from Colonial Times to the Present* (New York: Franklin Watts, 1975).

21. Ryan, *Womanhood in America*, p. 207.

22. Ann Oakley, *The Sociology of Housework* (New York: Random House, 1974), pp. 92–95.

23. Tilly and Scott, *Women, Work, and Family*, pp. 46, 58.

24. Margaret Mead, *Sex and Temperament in Three Primitive Societies* (New York: Dell, 1971), p. 55.

25. Oakley, *Sociology of Housework*, p. 93.

26. The 1979 figures for the typical 99.6-hour week of a housewife/mother, if paid at the minimum wage for each of her tasks, comes to $351.66 a week or $18,286.32 a year. New York *Daily News*, 25 February 1979.

27. Oakley, *Sociology of Housework*, pp. 136–41.

28. *Comment* II, I (September 1978): I, and Z. I. Giraldo and J. M. Weatherford, *Life Cycle and the American Family: Current Trends and Policy Implications* (Durham, N.C.: Duke University Institute of Policy Sciences and Public Affairs, Policy Paper #1 of the Center for the Study of Family and the State, 1978), pp. 3–1.

29. U.S. Bureau of the Census, *A Statistical Portrait of Women in the U.S.* (Washington, D.C.: Department of Commerce, Bureau of the Census, 1977), Current Population Reports, Special Studies Series P-23, no. 58, pp. 28, 30, 31.

30. Ibid., p. 45.

31. Department of Labor projections are that women will constitute 51.4 percent of the labor force by 1990. See Giraldo and Weatherford, *Life Cycle*, p. 3–10.

32. Ibid., pp. 3–7, 3–8.

33. Gutman, *The Black Family*, p. 530.

34. Giraldo and Weatherford, *Life Cycle*, pp. 1-1–1-15.

35. Stenton, *The English Woman*, p. 153. For the family patterns of preindustrial Europe, see Tilly and Scott, *Women, Work, and Family*, and Stone, *The Family, Sex, and Marriage*.

36. Tilly and Scott, *Women, Work, and Family*, p. 28.

37. Giraldo and Weatherford, *Life Cycle*, pp. 1-8, 1-16: Mary Jo Bane, *Here to Stay: The American Family in the Twentieth Century* (New York: Basic Books, 1976), p. 76.

38. Ad Hoc Women's Studies Committee against Sterilization Abuse, *Workbook on Sterilization and Sterilization Abuse* (Bronxville, N.Y.: Sarah Lawrence Publications, 1978); Committee for Abortion Rights and against Sterilization Abuse, *Women under Attack: Abortion, Sterilization Abuse, and Reproductive Freedom* (New York: CARASA, P.O. Box 124, Cathedral Station).

39. *Options*, the Newsletter of the Religious Coalition for Abortion Rights, published in Washington, D.C. (100 Maryland Ave., NE), regularly carries information of this kind.

INDEX